ISRAEL
in Pictures

Margaret J. Goldstein

Lerner Publications Company

Contents

Lerner Publishing Group realizes that current information and statistics quickly become out of date. To extend the usefulness of the Visual Geography Series, we developed www.vgsbooks.com, a website offering links to up-to-date information, as well as in-depth material, on a wide variety of subjects. All of the websites listed on www.vgsbooks.com have been carefully selected by researchers at Lerner Publishing Group. However, Lerner Publishing Group is not responsible for the accuracy or suitability of the material on any website other than <www.lernerbooks.com>. It is recommended that students using the Internet be supervised by a parent or teacher. Links on www.vgsbooks.com will be regularly reviewed and updated as needed.

Website address: www.lernerbooks.com

Lerner Publications Company
A division of Lerner Publishing Group
241 First Avenue North
Minneapolis, MN 55401 U.S.A.

web enhanced @ www.vgsbooks.com

Library of Congress Cataloging-in-Publication Data

Goldstein, Margaret J.
    Israel in pictures / revised and expanded by Margaret J. Goldstein.
      p. cm. — (Visual geography series)
    Summary: Text and illustrations present detailed information on the geography, history and government, economy, people, cultural life and society of traditional and modern Israel.
    ISBN: 0-8225-0935-0 (lib. bdg. : alk. paper)
    1. Israel—Pictorial works—Juvenile literature. [1. Israel.] I. Title. II. Visual geography series (Minneapolis, Minn.)
    DS108.5 .G63 2004
    956.94—dc21   2002152934

Manufactured in the United States of America
1 2 3 4 5 6 - JR - 09 08 07 06 05 04

INTRODUCTION

Israel, a small country in the heart of the Middle East, makes news daily. Unfortunately, the news coming out of Israel in recent years is mostly bad. Palestinian suicide bombers kill Israeli citizens. Israeli tanks and troops move into neighboring Palestinian towns. The world looks on with concern as the violence continues, wondering if this tiny country—a homeland for the Jewish people—will ever know peace.

Modern Israel was formed out of an international movement called Zionism. The movement began in the late 1800s, when European Jews set out to create a Jewish state in Israel, the ancient Jewish homeland. For centuries Jews had yearned to return to this holy land, a small sliver of territory on the eastern edge of the Mediterranean Sea. This land was to serve as a safe haven for Jews after a long history of oppression and discrimination. The Zionist dream was realized on May 14, 1948, when Israel declared its independence. Its history as a nation begins with that declaration.

But Israel actually has two histories, bridged by nearly two thousand years of Jewish exile. Israel's early history has been recorded in ancient sources, including the Hebrew Bible. The kingdom of Israel, the original Jewish nation, was established around 1000 B.C.E. Jerusalem was its capital city. About 135 C.E., Roman rulers—who had earlier extended their empire into Israel and other parts of the Middle East—expelled most of the Jews from their homeland. Jews scattered to various parts of the Middle East, North Africa, Spain, Northern Europe, and Rome itself—an action called the Diaspora (dispersal).

Renamed Palestine, Israel was held by many rulers—primarily the Romans, Arabs, and Ottoman Turks—for the next 1,800 years. Great Britain temporarily controlled the area after World War I (1914–1918). At that point, Zionist leaders stepped up their efforts to create a Jewish nation in their ancient homeland. Despite fierce opposition from the local Arab population, who did not want to see a Jewish state established in Palestine, the State of Israel was formally created in 1948.

Thus began the second stage of Israel's long history. This stage has been marked by tremendous success, including rich cultural and economic growth. Most important, Israel has provided a refuge for Jews from the around the world, who continue to flock there in great numbers. But modern Israel's short history has also been marked by persistent wars with surrounding Arab states. Thousands have been killed in these conflicts. Many peace negotiations have failed.

The Arab-Israeli conflict reached new heights in the early 2000s. Palestinian Arabs, living in Israeli-controlled territories bordering Israel, also claim Israel as their homeland. In their quest for independence, some Palestinians have resorted to bloody terror attacks against Israeli citizens. In response the Israeli army has cracked down hard on Palestinian towns. Hundreds have been killed on both sides. World leaders have tried to negotiate peace between the warring factions, but the hatred and bloodshed show little sign of slowing.

The State of Israel was founded to be a safe refuge from violence and hatred. Yet modern Israelis live with violence and terror on a daily basis. The Jews have long dreamed of a safe and peaceful life in Israel— "a land flowing with milk and honey" as described in the Bible. It remains to be seen when and whether that dream will be fully realized.

NOTE TO READER: Israel's history spans both ancient and modern times. Some books use the abbreviations B.C. ("before Christ") and A.D. (*anno Domini*, or "in the year of our Lord") to date ancient and modern events. This dating system is based on the birth of Jesus Christ, originally thought to have occurred in A.D. 1. Our book uses an alternative method that does not refer to Christ. We use the abbreviations B.C.E., or "before the common era," instead of B.C. We use C.E., or "of the common era," instead of A.D.

THE LAND

The State of Israel is a small country in the Middle East, located at the far eastern end of the Mediterranean Sea. Excluding disputed territories, it covers about 8,000 square miles (20,720 square kilometers), roughly the size of New Jersey. Approximately half desert, Israel measures about 265 miles (426 km) from north to south, about 70 miles (113 km) from east to west at its widest point, and just 10 miles (16 km) across at its narrowest point. Its neighbors are Lebanon to the north, Syria and Jordan to the east, and Egypt to the southwest. Along the west, Israel is bounded by the Mediterranean Sea.

Since its founding, Israel has been threatened and attacked numerous times by neighboring states. In the course of defending itself, Israel has captured additional territory: the Gaza Strip along the Mediterranean Sea, the West Bank of the Jordan River, including East Jerusalem, and the Golan Heights on the Syrian border. It also captured the Sinai Peninsula, which was later returned to Egypt. Gaza, the West

Bank, East Jerusalem, and the Golan Heights are called the disputed territories, or occupied territories. Their future remains uncertain.

▶ Topography

Geographically, Israel can be divided into four regions. The westernmost area, along the Mediterranean Sea, is called the coastal plain. It has sandy beaches, sand dunes, and low hills. The major cities of Haifa and Tel Aviv-Jaffa are located on the coastal plain. More than half of Israel's people live in this region. It is also rich agricultural land.

The Judeo-Galilean Highlands is a hilly region in north-central Israel. It runs from the Galilee area in the north to the Negev Desert in the south. This region includes Jerusalem, the disputed West Bank, and the largely Arab city of Nazareth. It also includes agricultural land and several mountain ranges. Mount Meron, 3,963 feet (1,208 meters), Israel's highest mountain, is located in the far north of this region.

The **Judeo-Galilean Highlands** feature rocky and hilly terrain.

Israel's easternmost area is called the Jordan Rift. It is part of the larger Great Rift Valley, which runs from Syria to southeastern Africa. This deep depression in the earth was formed millions of years ago. In Israel the rift encompasses the Jordan River, Lake Kinneret, and the Dead Sea.

The Negev Desert, Israel's driest region, occupies the southern portion of Israel. Sparsely populated, the rugged desert extends roughly from the city of Beersheba south to the city of Eilat. In the south, the desert features canyons, flatlands, plateaus, and craggy peaks. Israel has irrigated northern parts of the desert and brought large areas under cultivation. Farms there produce grain, corn, melons, alfalfa, citrus fruits, and other crops.

Rivers and Lakes

The longest river in Israel is the Jordan, which rises in the Golan Heights, runs southward through Lake Kinneret, and empties into the Dead Sea. Other rivers in Israel are much smaller. The Yarqon flows from the hills east of Tel Aviv-Jaffa on a 16-mile (26-km) course to the Mediterranean Sea. The Qarn, Qishon, and Hadera Rivers water northern Israel, and the Besor flows south of Beersheba during the winter rainy season.

With its shore at approximately 1,300 feet (396 m) below sea level, Israel's Dead Sea (actually a lake) is the lowest place on earth. It is also the saltiest body of water on earth—nine times saltier than the ocean. The Dead Sea has such a high salt content that few plants and animals can live in it, giving rise to the name. The water contains millions of tons of salt, magnesium, potassium, chlorine, and bromine.

Parts of **the Dead Sea** often crust over with salt deposits.

LEBANON

SYRIA

JUDEO-GALILEAN
HIGHLANDS

Qarn R.

Mount Meron ▲

GALILEE

MEDITERRANEAN
SEA

Mount
Carmel ▲

Qishon River

Lake
Kinneret
[Sea of Galilee]

Hadera River

Jordan River

Jordan Rift

COASTAL PLAIN

Yarqon R.

Old City
[Jerusalem]

JORDAN

DEAD
SEA

Masada ∴

Besor River

NEGEV DESERT

EGYPT

Sinai Peninsula

Gulf of Aqaba

Israel

Feet	Meters	
9843	3000	Mountains
6582	2000	Uplands
3281	1000	
1640	500	Lowlands

Elevation

N

—————— International border

- - - - - - Disputed border

∴ Archaeological site

▲ Mountain peak

0   40 Miles

0   40 KM

Lake Kinneret (also called Lake Tiberias or the Sea of Galilee) is located at the edge of the Golan Heights in northern Israel. Thirteen miles (21 km) long and 5 miles (8 km) wide, it is Israel's largest freshwater lake. It is an important source of freshwater for both drinking and irrigation. Northern Israel has several, much smaller lakes as well.

Climate

Israel has a Mediterranean climate, with long, hot, dry summers and short, cool, rainy winters. The weather varies from one region to the next, depending on altitude and distance from the sea. In August, Israel's hottest month, temperatures average 75°F (24°C) in northern Galilee and 90°F (32°C) in the Jordan Rift, although temperatures in the rift sometimes soar as high as 125°F (51°C). During the coolest month, January, Israel's temperatures range from 45°F (7°C) in northern Galilee to 60°F (15.5°C) in the Jordan Rift. In hilly areas, temperatures occasionally fall below freezing in winter.

Israel's sunny weather is ideal for the production of solar energy. Many Israelis use solar furnaces and solar water heaters in their homes and businesses. Organizations such as the Ben-Gurion National Solar Energy Center at Ben-Gurion University do research and testing on solar lighting, solar power generation, and other solar technologies.

Most of Israel's rain falls between November and April. Snow occasionally falls in the northern and central highlands. Northern Galilee receives about 40 inches (102 centimeters) of rain each year—the highest rainfall in the country. Eilat, at the southern tip of the Negev, receives only about 1 inch (2.5 cm) of rain each year. During spring and fall, hot, dry winds called khamsins sometimes blow through Israel from the deserts to the east. The winds carry dust and sand, which can impair visibility. Humidity can drop to an uncomfortable 0 percent at this time.

Flora and Fauna

In spring, Israel's hillsides and valleys come alive with wildflowers such as red anemones, white cyclamen, scarlet poppies, tulips, roses, and sunflowers. Other wild plants include honeysuckle, lotus, and papyrus. Pine, tamarisk, carob, oak, cypress, olive, date palm, fig, and almond trees also grow in Israel. Eucalyptus trees, imported from

Date palm trees

Once abundant in Israel, **Persian fallow deer** are nearly extinct. Israeli zoos are working to protect this endangered species.

Australia, are common. Millions of trees have been planted as part of a national reforestation program, operated by an organization called the Jewish National Fund. Altogether, about 2,500 plant species grow in Israel.

More than 500 bird species live in Israel. Some of them, such as storks and swallows, pass through on their annual migrations north and south. Coots, starlings, and ducks spend winters in Israel; turtledoves arrive for the summer. Songbirds such as warblers and goldcrests live in Israel year-round. Raptors include eagles, falcons, hawks, sparrow hawks, kestrels, and buzzards. Waterfowl include pelicans, egrets, purple herons, and storks. Wildcats, hyenas, jackals, foxes, wolves, boars, and gazelles live in the fertile Jordan River Valley and along the shores of the Dead Sea. Other land animals include ibexes, hares, badgers, and weasels.

Reptiles such as lizards and snakes populate the Dead Sea basin and the Negev Desert. Fish swim in Lake Kinneret and the Mediterranean Sea. The waters off Eilat, Israel's southernmost city, hold a famed coral reef, home to thousands of species of fish, coral, sponges, and shellfish. Sea turtles, sharks, and dolphins also swim off Israel's seacoast.

Natural Resources

Small and dry, Israel is not rich in natural resources. Its most valuable resources come from the Dead Sea and the Negev Desert, which contain minerals such as salt, copper, granite, and phosphate. Potash, a kind of salt that is used to make fertilizers, is the most important substance mined from the Dead Sea. Bromine, used in making drugs and other products, is another major Dead Sea resource.

Israel began drilling for oil in the 1940s, and small quantities of oil have been discovered, mostly under the Negev Desert and the coastal plain. But this oil meets only a small percentage of Israel's energy needs. Israel's Petroleum Commission thinks that significant oil reserves might still be found in the country, particularly offshore. In the 1990s, Israel stepped up oil exploration. It also has small deposits of natural gas and continues to search for more gas reserves.

Environmental Concerns

Like all industrial nations, Israel suffers from environmental problems. As the country's population has increased, its cities have become more crowded, cars and factories have created more air pollution, wilderness areas have shrunk, some animal and plant species have become endangered, and waterways have been dirtied. Israel is fighting these problems on several fronts.

In the area of nature conservation, Israel has established several hundred nature preserves and national parks. The Society for the Protection of Nature in Israel, established in 1953, offers environmental education and operates several nature centers around the country. Hunting is restricted in Israel, and the government has passed strict laws for the protection of wildlife and wilderness areas.

Israel has tackled air pollution by tightening emissions standards for motor vehicles and power plants. It has also launched programs and

laws dealing with solid waste disposal, recycling, and hazardous chemicals. Pollution continues to be a problem, however, especially in Israel's growing urban centers.

In 1993 Israel established the National River Administration to oversee cleanup of the country's most polluted waterways. Programs involve removal of solid and chemical wastes from river water, restoration of river ecosystems, development of riverside parks and recreational areas, wastewater treatment, and restrictions on future wastewater discharge.

In the arid Mideast, water itself is a precious commodity. Israel's few freshwater sources include Lake Kinneret, the Jordan River, a few smaller rivers, and underground water tables and springs. Water depletion, especially as Israel's population grows, is one of the nation's biggest environmental challenges.

Early in its history, Israel took steps to manage its scarce water resources. In 1964 the government completed the National Water Carrier, a network of pipes, canals, and pumping stations that carry water from the Jordan River and Lake Kinneret to dry southern Israel. The water is used for both drinking and irrigating farmland.

Israel has also pioneered programs in irrigation, wastewater treatment, and water storage and recycling. In the late 1900s, a huge reservoir of brackish (somewhat salty) water was discovered deep beneath the Negev Desert. Although this water is not safe for drinking, it has

been used to irrigate certain crops with great success. To ensure an adequate supply of freshwater for the future, Israel has started to build desalination facilities—processing plants where salt is removed from seawater. Finally, Israel hopes to import large amounts of freshwater from Turkey.

Water conservation is a key issue in Israel, due to the dry climate. Rivers, such as **the Jordan River,** provide water for drinking and irrigation.

Modern **Jerusalem** is a teeming metropolis. The city sprawls out over approximately 41 square miles (66 sq km).

Cities

About 91 percent of Israel's people live in cities and towns. Israel's largest cities are Jerusalem, Tel Aviv-Jaffa, and Haifa. Medium-sized cities include Eilat at the southern end of the Negev Desert, Beersheba in the north central Negev, and Nazareth in northern Israel.

Jerusalem, Israel's capital, is the nation's largest city, with a population of about 671,000. It is located on the edge of the Israeli-controlled West Bank, about 40 miles (64 km) east of the Mediterranean Sea. The ancient capital of the Israelites, Jerusalem has known many rulers over the centuries, including the Romans, Arabs, Ottoman Turks, and British. Evidence of their empires—roads, buildings, and monuments—are still seen throughout the city. One of the most fascinating parts of Jerusalem is the Old City, an ancient walled section.

Tourism has been Jerusalem's main industry for many years, with visitors of all faiths attracted to its religious and historic sites. In the early 2000s, Jerusalem became the focal point for increased

Arab-Israeli violence. Terror attacks such as suicide bombings severely slowed the tourist trade and damaged the city's economy.

Located on the Mediterranean Sea in central Israel, Tel Aviv-Jaffa is Israel's second largest city, with a population of roughly 350,000. It is the nation's manufacturing center, as well as the center of banking, publishing, technology, and other industries. It is also a major tourist destination. The city was originally two towns: Jaffa, a seaport dating to ancient times, and Tel Aviv, founded by European Jews in 1909. The two towns merged in 1950. Jaffa, the southwestern section of the city, was traditionally an Arab town, and it still has a large Arab population.

Built between the slopes of Mount Carmel and the banks of the Mediterranean Sea in northern Israel, Haifa is the nation's third largest city. It has a population of about 275,000. It is a major seaport and manufacturing center and holds numerous religious landmarks. Jews and Arabs have lived in the Haifa area since ancient times. The city was first used as a port in the 1850s.

A CAPITAL IN QUESTION

Tel Aviv served as Israel's capital during the first two years of independence, until Jerusalem became the nation's capital in 1950. But many foreign countries do not recognize Israel's claim to both the eastern and western sections of Jerusalem and do not want to place their embassies there. Thus, many countries maintain their embassies in Tel Aviv-Jaffa.

Situated on the central Mediterranean coast of Israel, **Tel Aviv-Jaffa** is the second largest city in the nation.

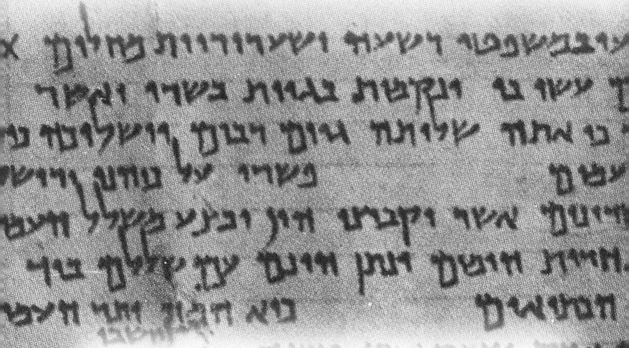

HISTORY AND GOVERNMENT

The Jewish presence in Israel began around 1800 B.C.E., when a shepherd named Abraham led a group of people across the Euphrates River from Mesopotamia (present-day Iraq and northeastern Syria) and into Canaan, as Israel was then called. At one site, Abraham and his people set up tents and dug seven wells. According to legend, they named the site Beersheba, which means "seven wells."

The Canaanites called the newcomers Ibrim (Hebrews), which might have meant "people from the other side of the river," although the origin of the name is uncertain. Later, the Hebrews came to be called Israelites—a term for descendants of Abraham's grandson Jacob, who was also called Israel. Nomads without a territory of their own, the Israelites wandered within Canaan for generations, until a famine struck the area in the 1400s B.C.E.

The Israelites then migrated into Egypt, where after a time they were enslaved by the Egyptians. During the 1200s B.C.E., a man named Moses led the Israelites out of slavery, an event known as the Exodus.

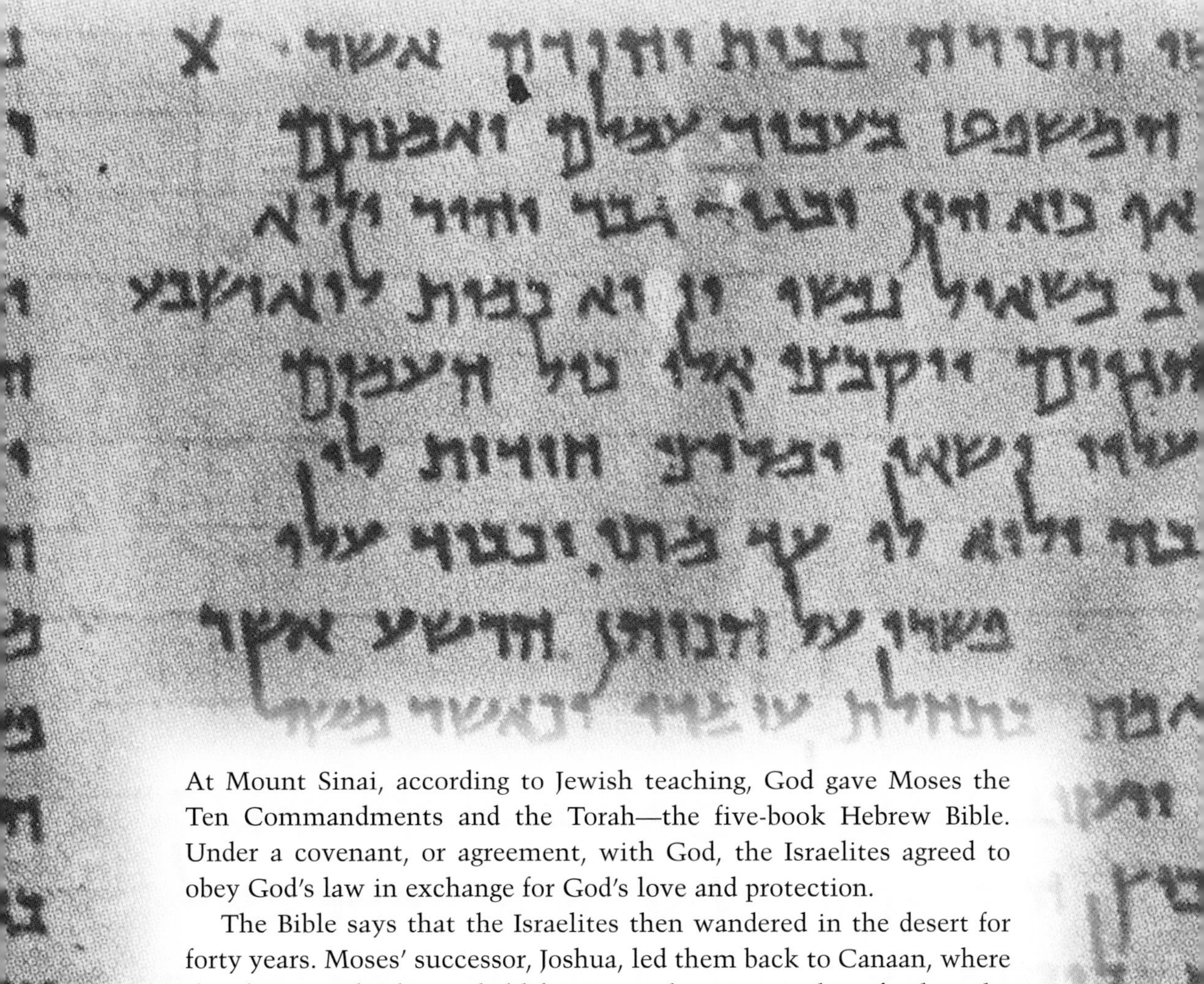

X · אשר   יותרית בצות יותרים יו

ואשכן בצבר עעים ואתשמה

אף בוא ותן ובגר   גבר ותדר ילוא

בי באשיאו נצאו יו וא כבות לואריצבע

אתוים יוקבצ אלי טל העבשה

עודו יאשן ובארצ   חורות לו

את ולוא לי עי פת, ובצרך עלו

בשין עו ודנותן. חדשע אשר

בדאשי עו צלת לואראנף אשר

At Mount Sinai, according to Jewish teaching, God gave Moses the Ten Commandments and the Torah—the five-book Hebrew Bible. Under a covenant, or agreement, with God, the Israelites agreed to obey God's law in exchange for God's love and protection.

The Bible says that the Israelites then wandered in the desert for forty years. Moses' successor, Joshua, led them back to Canaan, where they began to lead a settled life. Grouped into a number of tribes, the Israelites united only in times of war and crisis. For about two hundred years, they fought various peoples in Canaan, including the Canaanites and the Philistines.

The Philistines presented a powerful threat, forcing the Israelites to band together more tightly than they had before. They united under a monarchy and chose Saul as their king. Saul's successor, David, defeated the Philistines around 1000 B.C.E. He then established Jerusalem as the capital of the kingdom of Israel. David was succeeded by his son, Solomon. A wise and diplomatic ruler, Solomon built a great temple in

Jerusalem, later called the First Temple. After Solomon's death, feuding tribes split the kingdom into Israel in the north and Judah in the south. Citizens in both regions came to be known as Jews, a variation of the Hebrew term *yehudi*, which means "citizen of Judah."

Invasions and Conquests

In 721 B.C.E., the Assyrians—who were extending their rule westward from present-day Iraq—conquered the northern kingdom of Israel. Judah remained independent, until it was conquered by the Babylonians in 586 B.C.E. They destroyed Jerusalem, including King Solomon's temple, and exiled many Jews to Babylonia. But the Jews did not forget Jerusalem. About fifty years later, when Cyrus the Great of Persia conquered the Babylonians, he permitted the Jews to return to Judah and restore their former capital. The returning Jews rebuilt their temple, called the Second Temple in modern times.

The Persian Empire fell to the Greeks, under the leadership of Alexander the Great, in 331 B.C.E. Alexander, like the Persian rulers before him, respected the Jewish belief in one God. He granted Jews religious freedom as well as a considerable amount of self-government. After Alexander's death, his successors, the Ptolemies of Egypt and the Seleucids of Syria, continued to allow the Jews religious freedom. Eventually, though, the Seleucids tried to impose their culture and religion on the Jews.

Under the leadership of the Maccabee brothers, the Jews revolted in the 160s B.C.E. and set up an independent state in Judah. The Jewish state lasted less than a century, however. In 63 B.C.E., the Roman general Pompey the Great conquered Judah for the Roman Empire. The Romans renamed the country Judea.

Roman rule was harsh, and the Jews rebelled against Rome in 66 C.E. Thousands of Jews died in the four-year war that followed, including

KEYS TO THE PAST

The Dead Sea Scrolls are ancient manuscripts that contain copies of biblical books, as well as Jewish prayers, hymns, legends, laws, and religious discussions. The scrolls were probably made by the Essenes, members of an ancient Jewish sect. The earliest scrolls date to the 200s B.C.E. A Bedouin shepherd boy discovered the first scrolls in 1947, preserved in a cave in earthenware jars. Altogether, more than eight hundred scrolls have been found. Most of them were written in Hebrew on leather or papyrus. They are housed at the Shrine of the Book at the Israel Museum in Jerusalem. To find out more about the Dead Sea Scrolls, go to vgsbooks.com.

Reminders of Roman rule, such as this ancient **aqueduct,** dot the Israeli landscape. The Roman Empire ruled Israel for more than six hundred years.

nearly one thousand Zealots, members of a militant Jewish group. It is said that the Zealots, besieged in a fortress called Masada, committed suicide rather than surrender to the Romans. After the fighting was over, Jerusalem was nearly destroyed. But several Jewish settlements escaped destruction.

In 132 C.E., Simon Bar Kokhba led Jewish fighters in a final effort to throw off the Roman yoke. After three years of war, the Romans broke Jewish resistance. Determined that the Jews would never again rebel, the Roman emperor Hadrian expelled most of the Jews from Jerusalem. Judea was renamed Palestine, derived from the word Philistine.

The scattering of the Jews, the Jewish Diaspora, would last for more than 1,800 years. First in the Mediterranean area and later in Europe, the Jews wandered, eventually settling throughout the world. Often victims of discrimination, they nevertheless clung to their faith, their customs, and their history—and to the hope of returning one day to their homeland.

Back in Palestine

For the next five hundred years, Palestine remained in Roman hands. First it was part of the Roman Empire, then it belonged to the Eastern Roman, or Byzantine, Empire. The area was home to a variety of peoples, including small groups of Jews who remained after the Roman expulsion. It was also home to Christians, members of a new religion that had emerged in Palestine during the first century C.E. This faith was based on the teachings of Jesus of Nazareth, born in Judea around 6 B.C.E. and considered by his followers to be the long-awaited savior. Gradually, Christianity spread throughout the Roman Empire and Europe.

In 637 C.E., Arab armies, based on the Arabian Peninsula southeast of Palestine, conquered Palestine, Egypt, Syria, and other parts of the Middle East. The Arab conquerors were Muslims, people who practiced the Islamic faith. This faith is based on the teachings of the prophet Muhammad. Its holy book is called the Quran. Gradually, Islam spread throughout the Middle East, becoming the major religion in the region.

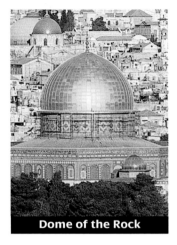

Dome of the Rock

In Jerusalem Arab rulers renewed the city. They built impressive structures such as the Dome of the Rock, a splendid gold-topped shrine. Palestine flourished under Arab rule, but the Arabs treated the Jews and Christians there like second-class citizens. They suffered frequent discrimination during this era.

Power changed hands yet again in the late 1000s, when European armies swept into the Middle East, in a campaign known as the Crusades. By then, Christianity had become the dominant religion in Europe. Many European Christians viewed Palestine—Jesus' birthplace—as a holy

During **the Crusades,** European Christians invaded and briefly conquered Jerusalem.

land. They wanted to claim this land as their own. The Christian armies had some initial success, capturing Jerusalem in 1099. They failed to establish a permanent presence in Palestine, however, and their short-lived Kingdom of Jerusalem collapsed in 1187.

The Arabs regained control of the region and held it until 1258, when the Mongols invaded. Warriors from eastern Asia, the Mongols destroyed the important Arab city of Baghdad, ending Arab power. The Mamelukes—a group of Asian slave/soldiers who had risen to power in Egypt—ruled Palestine from the mid-1200s until 1517. In that year, a group called the Ottoman Turks took the Middle East from the Mamelukes. The Ottomans developed a powerful empire that lasted for several centuries. All the while, through the succession of foreign rulers, Arab Muslims made up the majority of the region's population, with smaller numbers of Jews, Christians, and members of other faiths.

The Growth of Zionism

Although some Jews remained in the Middle East, most had scattered throughout the world. Over the centuries, Jewish communities had developed in many nations, with large concentrations in Eastern Europe. In many places, the Jews endured ongoing persecution, discrimination, and violence. In Russia, for instance, soldiers massacred thousands of Jews in organized campaigns called pogroms. Starting in the late 1800s, great numbers of Jews began to flee Europe, most of them heading for the United States, with smaller numbers moving to Palestine and elsewhere.

Around this time, the Zionist movement took hold in Europe. This movement set as its goal the return of the Jewish people to Israel, sometimes also called Zion. Zionists viewed Israel as the Jews' rightful homeland. They also saw a Jewish-run state as the only remedy to the problems of the Jewish people. The Zionists felt that anti-Semitism, discrimination against Jews, would never be eliminated altogether—the only solution was for Jews to have a nation of their own. In 1897 Theodor Herzl, an Austrian Jew and author of *The Jewish State*, founded the World Zionist Organization to seek political support for this plan.

The Zionists bought land in Palestine in the early 1900s and established farms and settlements there. But Arabs also lived in Palestine—and had for centuries—and they were not happy about large-scale Jewish immigration to the area. What's more, the Zionists purchased many lands from absentee landlords, wealthy landowners who lived elsewhere. The Arab peasants who

"If you will it, it is no dream."

—Theodor Herzl

Theodor Herzl

had previously farmed the land were forced to move. Anti-Zionist anger grew. By 1911 Arabs in Palestine had organized opposition to the influx of Jews.

The Arabs, long under Ottoman rule, also desired an independent homeland in the Middle East. During World War I, Great Britain and its allies, including France and the United States, fought against Germany, the Ottoman Empire, and several other nations. Great Britain promised the Arabs independence after the war in exchange for their support of the Allies. In another commitment—the Balfour Declaration of 1917—Britain promised the Jews, whose help it also wanted in the war effort, a Jewish "national home" in Palestine. Thus, when the war ended, the British felt obligated to ensure Arab independence *and* to help create a Jewish state in Palestine.

Visit vgsbooks.com for links where you can learn more about Zionism (including Theodor Herzl and the World Zionist Organization), a detailed history of the Israeli-Palestinian conflict, and more.

 ## The Seeds of Conflict

Great Britain took control of Palestine and other parts of the Middle East in 1920. Under terms established by the League of Nations, Palestine was called a "mandated territory." Great Britain was put in charge of the territory until the Palestinian people were prepared for self-government. In 1921 Great Britain granted partial self-government to a section of Palestine called Transjordan (modern-day Jordan). The rest of Palestine remained under British rule.

The Balfour Declaration had stated that a return of the Jews to Palestine should not negatively affect the native Arab population. In keeping with that goal, Great Britain set strict yearly limits on how many Jews could immigrate.

When the anti-Jewish Nazis came to power in Germany in 1933, Jewish immigration to Palestine rose sharply. Fearful of Jewish domination, the Palestinian Arabs revolted against British control a number of times between 1936 and 1939. The British set forth several proposals for partitioning, or dividing, the land, all of which the Arabs rejected. In 1939, hoping to appease the Arabs, Britain set even stricter limits on the number of Jews who could immigrate to Palestine.

By then World War II (1939–1945) had broken out in Europe. During the course of the war, the Nazis killed about six million European Jews. This mass murder, called the Holocaust, evoked world sympathy for European Jews and the Zionist cause. Nevertheless, Britain continued to limit Jewish immigration into Palestine during and after the war. Survivors of the Nazi death camps had no homes to return to. Many made their way into Palestine illegally.

Tension between Jews and Arabs within Palestine continued to intensify. In 1947 Britain declared the mandate established after World War I unworkable and asked the United Nations (UN) to help solve the Palestinian problem. The UN Special Commission on Palestine recommended that the region be divided into an Arab state and a Jewish state, with Jerusalem put under international control. Zionists accepted the plan—finally the world had recognized their right to a state in Israel. But the Arabs refused to accept any partition plan. They were all the more displeased by the fact that the plan called for the Jewish minority to receive 55 percent of the land in question—although most of the Jewish portion was desert.

The Fight for Independence

In accordance with the UN plan, Britain withdrew from Palestine on May 14, 1948. On the same day, Zionist leaders proclaimed the creation of the independent state of Israel. The Arab states of Egypt, Jordan, Syria, Lebanon, Iraq, Saudi Arabia, and Yemen promptly declared war against Israel. The surrounding nations outnumbered Israel in population 40 to 1 and in area 400 to 1. To face the combined enemy armies, including Jordan's famed (and British-led) Arab Legion, the Israeli army, the Haganah, had only about 35,000 troops.

David Ben-Gurion, Israel's first prime minister, reads the Declaration of the Establishment of the State of Israel.

To further complicate Israel's position, the state was bordered on three sides by enemy nations. Not only was it impossible to patrol the borders adequately, but Israel was only 10 miles (16 km) wide in places, making the new nation vulnerable and leaving little room for retreat. The Arabs initially gained the upper hand, besieging Jerusalem. But when the Israelis broke the siege, the tide of the war began to turn.

When the fighting ended, in addition to its own territory, Israel held about half the area the UN had planned for a new Arab state. Egypt and Jordan held the rest of Palestine, and the city of Jerusalem was split between Jordan and Israel. For the Jewish people, the Diaspora had finally ended, but for the Palestinian Arabs it had just begun. Many fled their lands in 1948 to escape the fighting or to make way for Arab troops. Within the first three months of Israel's creation, more than 600,000 Arabs left the country, mainly for Jordan and other Mideast nations. About 160,000 remained in Israel.

While most of the world recognized the new State of Israel, the Arab nations refused to do so. They promptly imposed a strict economic boycott of Israel and cut off all communications with Israel. Although Arab guerrilla fighters continued to raid Israel's borders, the nation was no longer formally at war. It could turn its attention to internal development. The new nation held its first election in January 1949, with voters choosing a Knesset, or parliament. Zionist leaders Chaim Weizmann and David Ben-Gurion became Israel's first president and prime minister, respectively.

Jews from around the world flocked to the new Jewish homeland. The Law of Return, passed in 1950, granted automatic Israeli citizenship to any Jew who wanted it. The Israeli population grew rapidly, as did industry, agriculture, communication systems, educational institutions, and other aspects of the new society.

Renewed Warfare

Peace was not to last. Border clashes increased between Arab guerrilla fighters and Israeli troops, especially along the frontier with Egypt. On October 29, 1956, Israel launched a military campaign against Egyptian bases in the Sinai Peninsula. British and French leaders helped orchestrate the action, because Egypt had recently seized the Suez Canal, a strategic waterway on the western edge of the Sinai, from its British and French owners.

While British and French ships headed toward the northern end of the canal, Israel's army crossed the Sinai Desert, knocking out one-third of Egypt's army and destroying Egyptian military bases. Within a few days, the Israelis had reached the canal. With strong pressure from the United States, the parties agreed to a United Nations–brokered cease-fire. Israeli forces withdrew from Egypt in early 1957. The UN also sent peacekeeping forces to the Israeli-Egyptian border and the Gaza Strip, a small piece of land at the northeastern edge of the Sinai.

Clashes along Israel's borders continued in the 1960s, especially with Syria and Jordan. In the spring of 1967, Egypt demanded removal of UN forces from Sinai and the Gaza Strip, and the UN complied. The Egyptian army then entered Sinai and blockaded the Strait of Tiran, at the northern end of the Red Sea. This action halted Israel's vital shipping trade with nations to the east. Fearing an Arab attack, Israel mobilized its forces and on June 5, 1967, simultaneously attacked Egypt and Syria. Jordan immediately joined its Arab neighbors in the fight with Israel.

But Arab air forces were destroyed before they could leave their bases. Israeli ground forces swept halfway to Damascus in Syria and all the way to the Suez Canal. After just six days of fighting, Israel held the Sinai Peninsula and Gaza, the West Bank of the Jordan River, East Jerusalem, and the Golan Heights. A cease-fire was declared, but the seeds of a new conflict had been sown.

The captured territories were by then home to more than one million Arabs—people who had no wish to be ruled by Israel. Many of these people were Palestinians who had left their homes with the creation of Israel in 1948. The Palestinians desired a homeland of their own. A new group, the Palestinian Liberation Organization (PLO), took the lead in the movement for Palestinian independence. Its goals were twofold. In addition to fighting for independence, the PLO wanted to eliminate Israel altogether. The organization used guerrilla tactics and terrorism, including bombings and hijackings, to call attention to its cause. Starting in the late 1960s, PLO guerrillas struck out at Israelis and other Jews around the world.

One Step Forward, Two Steps Back

After a few years of calm, the armies of Syria and Egypt attacked Israel in October 1973, hoping to regain the territories they had lost during the Six-Day War. The attack took place on Yom Kippur, the holiest day of the Jewish calendar. The Israelis were caught off guard. Fierce air battles took place in the skies over Israel. Egyptian ground forces crossed the Suez Canal into the Sinai Desert. The United States and the Soviet Union intervened and negotiated an end to the fighting. With U.S. secretary of state Henry Kissinger acting as mediator, Egypt and Syria signed cease-fire agreements with Israel in 1974.

The Yom Kippur War hurt Israel in several ways: The Israeli military suffered heavy losses of both soldiers and equipment during the fighting. Israel's economy also suffered once the conflict had ended.

Many people blamed Prime Minister Golda Meir for Israel's lack of preparedness for the war and the troubles that followed. She resigned her position in April 1974.

Golda Meir

The Israeli economy eventually recovered, and growth continued. Tourism was an increasingly important industry, with more than one million foreign visitors traveling to Israel each year, many of them American Jews. Needing constant defense, Israel purchased great amounts of weapons from the United States. It also made lucrative trade agreements with other nations. As the economy grew, Israeli cultural and educational institutions also flourished. New Jewish citizens continued to arrive in Israel from around the world.

In 1977 Israeli prime minister Menachem Begin and Egyptian president Anwar Sadat took a bold step. They agreed to meet in Jerusalem to negotiate peace and to settle the Palestinian issue. Although there was great enthusiasm for the Sadat visit, discussions between the two states made little progress. U.S. president Jimmy Carter then offered to help the peace process along. He invited Begin and Sadat to meet together at Camp David, the presidential retreat in Maryland.

Held in September 1978, the Camp David meetings led to a peace treaty between the two nations. The treaty, signed on March 26, 1979, called for Israel to withdraw from the Sinai in several phases. In return, Egypt agreed to recognize the State of Israel. The two countries established full diplomatic relations as well as economic agreements.

The Camp David Accords were signed in 1979 by Egyptian president Anwar Sadat, U.S. president Jimmy Carter, and Israeli prime minister Menachem Begin *(from left to right)*.

Israel's Changing Boundaries

This series of maps shows how various treaties, wars, and disputes have changed Israel's official boundaries over the decades.

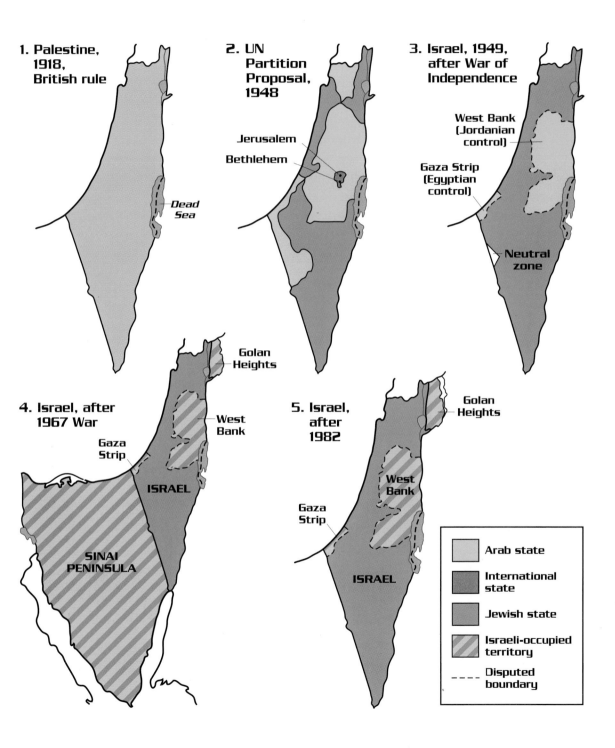

1. Palestine, 1918, British rule

Dead Sea

2. UN Partition Proposal, 1948

Jerusalem

Bethlehem

3. Israel, 1949, after War of Independence

West Bank (Jordanian control)

Gaza Strip (Egyptian control)

Neutral zone

4. Israel, after 1967 War

Golan Heights

West Bank

Gaza Strip

ISRAEL

SINAI PENINSULA

5. Israel, after 1982

Golan Heights

West Bank

Gaza Strip

ISRAEL

Arab state

International state

Jewish state

Israeli-occupied territory

Disputed boundary

The treaty also called for a five-year transition period, after which some form of Palestinian self-rule would be established on the West Bank and in the Gaza Strip. Sadat paid a high price for his willingness to recognize Israel, however. Egyptian militants, opposed to Sadat's negotiations with Israel, assassinated him in 1981. By 1982 Israeli troops had fully withdrawn from the Sinai.

Still the fighting continued, this time on Israel's northern border. In the early 1970s, a branch of the PLO had taken control of the southern part of Lebanon. From there, the PLO launched guerrilla and rocket attacks on northern Israeli settlements. Israel fought back, starting in the late 1970s. On June 6, 1982, Israel began Operation Peace for Galilee, attacking PLO fighters in southern Lebanon and chasing them to Beirut, the Lebanese capital. Although the PLO was defeated and temporarily left Lebanon, Israel found itself embroiled in a vicious Lebanese civil war. Opposition to involvement in Lebanon grew within Israel, and the military withdrew most of its forces from Lebanon in the summer of 1985.

One infamous PLO attack took place at the 1972 Summer Olympic Games in Munich, Germany. During the event, Palestinian terrorists broke into the Olympic Village, killing two Israeli athletes and taking nine more hostage. The Palestinians demanded the release of more than two hundred Arabs imprisoned in Israel. In a shootout with German police at the Munich airport, five terrorists, one police officer, and all the Israeli hostages were killed.

The Disputed Territories

In the late 1980s, the Arab-Israel conflict centered most heavily on the West Bank and the Gaza Strip. Since the Six-Day War, Palestinians in these areas had been governed by Israel's Ministry of Defense. They were able to hold jobs in Israel, but often these jobs were low paying. Many Palestinians were refugees who had left their homes during the war for Israeli independence. Some of them lived in UN-operated refugee camps.

The Israeli government gave the Palestinians limited political independence, such as the right to elect local officials. But, by and large, their freedom was restricted. The Israeli government was suspicious of Palestinian leaders, particular those with ties to the PLO and other extremist groups. To discourage terrorist activity, the Israeli army sometimes made mass arrests in the disputed territories. Soldiers made extensive searches and imposed strict curfews and other restrictions in towns that were suspected to house terrorists.

A refugee camp on the outskirts of Jericho on the West Bank. Many Palestinians live in similar settlements throughout the West Bank and Gaza.

Adding more fuel to the conflict, in the late 1970s, small groups of religious Jews had begun to settle in the disputed territories, establishing small towns and farms there. Some settlers argued that their right to the land dated to biblical times. Often, violence broke out between settlers and Palestinians. A number of people were killed on both sides.

In late 1987, Palestinian discontent erupted in an *intifada*, or uprising, against the Israeli military administration. Palestinians boycotted Israeli goods, withheld taxes, and made other protests against Israel. Many young Palestinians hurled stones, bricks, and firebombs at Israeli troops. The soldiers retaliated with force, including gunfire. Many Palestinians lost their lives in clashes with Israeli soldiers.

Within Israel, opinions about the disputed territories differed widely. Many Israelis favored a "land for peace" deal. They were willing to give back lands captured in 1967 in exchange for peace with the Palestinians. Other Israelis opposed giving up any land. Some thought that returning the land would not bring about peace and would only weaken Israel. Others thought that God had given the land to the Jewish people. They noted that Jews had lived there for thousands of years—longer than the Palestinians.

From Negotiation to Bloodshed

In 1992 Israel's liberal-leaning Labor Party came to power, with Yitzhak Rabin named prime minister. Rabin had campaigned on a peace platform. In secret, in late 1992 and early 1993, his government carried out peace negotiations with representatives of the PLO in Oslo, Norway. On September 13, 1993, Rabin signed a groundbreaking agreement with PLO leader Yasser Arafat. Known as the Oslo Accords, the agreement was sealed with a ceremony at the White House with U.S. president Bill Clinton.

Under the accords, the PLO agreed to renounce terrorism and to recognize Israel's right to statehood. Israel agreed to partial self-rule for the Palestinians and gradual withdrawal of Israeli troops from portions

Israeli foreign minister **Shimon Peres** *(right)* received the Nobel Peace Prize for his diplomatic efforts to reconcile Israeli and Palestinian differences.

of the occupied territories. Other unresolved issues were left for future discussions. For their efforts, Arafat, Rabin, and Israeli foreign minister Shimon Peres were awarded the Nobel Peace Prize in 1994.

Although much of the world applauded the Oslo Accords, many within Israel were outraged by the agreement. Claiming that God had given the disputed territories to the Jews, an Israeli religious extremist assassinated Rabin at a peace rally in November 1995. Shimon Peres succeeded Rabin as prime minister. He vowed to continue the peace process.

In keeping with the Oslo Accords, Israeli troops began to withdraw from the disputed territories in the fall of 1995. The Palestinians held elections in 1996, and Yasser Arafat was chosen president of a new governing body, the Palestinian National Authority. The authority prepared to take charge of law enforcement, education, health care, taxation, and other areas of Palestinian self-governance.

But the Oslo agreement soon fell apart. Terrorism escalated, with new Palestinian groups such as Hamas and Hizballah calling for the destruction of Israel. Some groups called their cause a jihad, or holy war on behalf of Islam. They attacked Israelis with suicide bombings and other terror tactics. The new Palestinian Authority made few efforts to fight the terrorism. Dissatisfied with their government's inability to prevent the attacks, Israeli voters elected Benjamin Netanyahu prime minister in 1996. He promised security for Israel and abandoned the peace process. He also allowed new Jewish settlements to be built on the West Bank and in East Jerusalem, further angering Palestinians.

As the violence continued, however, Netanyahu finally agreed to renewed peace talks with Yasser Arafat. This time President Clinton mediated the discussions, which resulted in the Wye River Accord of 1998. Netanyahu's successor, Ehud Barak, continued peace talks, again with President Clinton acting as mediator. But the discussions ended bitterly when Arafat rejected Barak's offer for control of most but not all of the West Bank and the Gaza Strip.

Benjamin Netanyahu

Once again, Israelis lost faith in the peace process. In February 2001, Ariel Sharon was elected prime minister of Israel. A former general and defense minister, he promised to crack down hard on terrorists. He also charged that Yasser Arafat, rather than trying to stop terrorists, was in fact collaborating with them.

Violence reached new heights in 2002, with a series of suicide bombings in Israeli buses, cafes, and markets. Hundreds of Israelis were killed. The nation tightened security everywhere—in nightclubs, theaters, and marketplaces, along roads, even on beaches. In response to the attacks, Sharon sent his army into Palestinian towns and refugee camps in an effort to flush out terrorists. In the process, many Palestinians were killed by Israeli troops. The United States intervened to try to end the violence, as did several Middle Eastern nations—but the terror attacks continued. In June 2002, Israel began

Israeli bomb squads became very busy at the beginning of the twenty-first century, due to increased suicide bombings.

to build a security wall around the West Bank, in hopes of keeping suicide bombers from getting into Israel.

The Government

Israel is a democratic nation. It has never written a constitution, but it has passed a series of "Basic Laws" that outline governmental operation. Citizens are represented by a unicameral (one-house) legislature called the Knesset, which passes laws for the nation. The 120 Knesset members are elected to four-year terms. Every Israeli citizen over age eighteen can vote in national elections.

Israel has a parliamentary system of government, similar to that of many democratic countries in Europe. Under this system, voters do not directly elect the prime minister, the head of the executive branch of government. Instead, voters elect the Knesset, and the Knesset chooses the prime minister—usually the head of the leading political party in the Knesset. (In 1996, 1999, and 2001, Israel held direct elections for prime minister but then returned to the previous system.) The prime minister selects cabinet members, who oversee ministries such as education, health care, defense, and finance. These ministers, too, are usually leading members of the Knesset.

The Knesset also elects a president, who serves a seven-year term. Unlike the president of the United States, however, the Israeli president is not the head of government. His or her duties are largely ceremonial, such as receiving foreign diplomats.

Under the Israeli system, voters do not cast ballots for individual Knesset members. Instead citizens vote for a slate of candidates put forward by each political party. The number of candidates a party sends

The **Knesset** comprises the legislative branch of the Israeli government.

to the Knesset depends on the percentage of votes it receives in the national election. Israel's most prominent political parties are the liberal Labor Party and the conservative Likud Party. Many other parties represent specific groups of voters, such as Orthodox Jews, Russian immigrants, and Muslim Israelis. Labor and Likud usually win the most seats in the Knesset, but more than a dozen other parties generally hold seats as well.

Israel has two kinds of courts—civil (nonreligious) and religious. Civil courts include a supreme court, district courts, and municipal, or city, courts. These courts rule on criminal cases, contract disputes, labor issues, and other legal matters. Most personal legal matters, such as divorces, are handled by religious courts. Israel's Jews, Muslims, Christians, and other religious groups each have their own religious courts.

Israel is divided into six smaller districts—the Central, Haifa, Jerusalem, Northern, Southern, and Tel Aviv districts—which oversee local and regional matters. A commissioner, appointed by the federal government, heads each district and reports to the national minister of the interior. People also elect city and regional officials to deal with other matters of local government.

MANDATORY SERVICE

Most Israeli men and unmarried women must serve in the nation's military, called the Israel Defense Forces (IDF). Recruits are drafted at age eighteen—men for three years, women for two years. Many immigrants are also required to serve, depending upon their age and family status. After their initial service, men serve in reserve units until age fifty-one. Unmarried women serve in the reserves until age twenty-four. Some Israelis are exempt from military service, primarily ultra-Orthodox Jews studying in religious seminaries.

THE PEOPLE

From about 800,000 people in 1948, Israel's population has grown to approximately six million, including Israelis living in the disputed territories of East Jerusalem, the Golan Heights, Gaza, and the West Bank. Israel does not have a high birth rate. The figure is 2.9 children per woman, compared to more than 4 children per woman in many neighboring Middle Eastern states. Although Israel's birth rate is low, its population is augmented by immigration. Between 1990 and 2000, about one million people immigrated to Israel. Its population is expected to grow to about seven million by 2010.

Israel's population is diverse, in part because Israel offers nearly automatic citizenship to Jews from around the world. As a result, Jewish immigrants regularly arrive in Israel from other Middle Eastern nations, North Africa, Europe, North and South America, and other areas. Since the 1980s, the largest influx of immigrants has come from the former Soviet Union. Non-Jews may also move to Israel, but for them acquiring citizenship is a formal legal process, just as it is in the

United States. Most immigrants arrive knowing little Hebrew—Israel's primary language. They bring a variety of languages, foods, traditions, and styles of dress to their new homeland. About 40 percent of Israel's people were born in other countries.

Adding to this diversity is Israel's religious mix. Most Israelis are Jewish, but Muslims, Christians, and members of other faiths also live in Israel. Although Israel is a Jewish state, its law guarantees freedom of religion for every citizen. Each religious community is allowed to observe its weekly Sabbath and its holidays. Religious councils and courts govern the personal affairs of each religious group.

Jewish Israelis

Jews make up about 78 percent of the Israeli population. While the majority of them were born in Israel, others come from more than seventy different nations worldwide. Native-born Israelis are nicknamed sabras, after the country's prickly pear cactus. The immigrants are called *olim*.

Jewish Israelis celebrate holidays with special meals.

Traditionally, Israel's Jews have been divided into three groups, depending on their ancestry. Ashkenazim are descendants of European Jews—mostly immigrants from Poland, Germany, and Russia who arrived in Israel in the early and mid-twentieth century. Some Ashkenazim immigrated to North or South America before moving to Israel. Ashkenazim made up the majority of Israel's founding population.

Sephardim are descendants of Spanish and Portuguese Jews who, because they refused to convert to Christianity, were expelled from Spain and Portugal in the late 1400s. These Jews scattered throughout the Mediterranean region, settling in North Africa, the Middle East, the Balkans, Turkey, and western Europe. Although some Sephardim were already living in Israel prior to its founding, most arrived after 1948. Their original language was Ladino, a mixture of Hebrew and Spanish.

A third category, Oriental Jews, are often grouped together with the Sephardim. These Jews came to Israel from other parts of the Middle East and southwest Asia, countries such as Yemen, Afghanistan, Iraq, Iran, and India. Unlike the Sephardim and Ashkenazim, their ancestors never lived in Europe. The Orientals generally spoke Arabic before their arrival in Israel. Most arrived in the 1950s. Within Israel, distinctions between the Sephardim and Orientals are blurry because of their similar Eastern backgrounds.

Early in Israel's history, tensions arose between the Ashkenazi community and the Sephardim and Orientals. The European Jews, the original majority, were Western in their outlook, culture, and technology. They were generally better educated, wealthier, and more modern than the Sephardim and Orientals. They were the nation's founders and first leaders. Initially, the Orientals and Sephardim were treated somewhat like second-class citizens. With their Eastern dress and customs, they did not fit in with the Israeli mainstream. They rarely rose to powerful positions in government or business.

Gradually, though, the distinctions between Ashkenazim, Sephardim, and Oriental Jews have become less pronounced. More and more Jews are Israeli-born. They grow up embracing the customs of modern Israel as well as those of their ancestral homelands. In addition, Jews continue to arrive in Israel from other places, particularly the former Soviet Union. Significant numbers have also come from famine-stricken Ethiopia. Another influx

JUDAISM—THE BASIS OF ISRAELI LIFE

Israel was founded as a Jewish state, and the majority of Israelis are Jewish. Jews believe in one God. Their basic laws and teachings come from the five books of the Torah—said to be given from God to Moses at Mount Sinai. Other teachings are found in the Talmud, an ancient book of law. Jewish houses of worship are called synagogues. Religious leaders are called rabbis. At age thirteen, Jewish boys receive a bar mitzvah. After this ceremony, a boy is considered a man. Some Jewish girls celebrate a similar coming-of-age ritual, called a bat mitzvah.

Judaism has evolved over the centuries. In modern times, many Jews do not follow strict Jewish teachings but still observe religious holidays and traditions. The three main branches of Judaism—from the most observant to the most liberal—are Orthodox, Conservative, and Reform.

Some Jewish males in Israel wear skullcaps called *kippas* or yarmulkes. These small hats are worn to honor God.

comes from Argentina, where Jews have recently struggled with economic distress and anti-Semitism. These new arrivals bring even more variety to Israel's already diverse population. As old distinctions fade out, new ones are created. Israel's ethnic makeup is constantly in flux.

In addition to ethnic divisions, Jewish Israelis often split along religious lines. Some Jewish Israelis (about 20 percent) are Orthodox or ultra-Orthodox. These Israelis adhere strictly to Jewish teachings. They favor a religious state that operates according to the laws of the Torah—the Hebrew Bible. Although these Jews constitute a minority of Israel's people, they wield considerable political power. Most Israeli Jews are religiously observant but not Orthodox. Some are not observant at all. Nonobservant Israelis favor a modern democracy, with a minimum of religious intrusion on daily life.

Orthodox Jewish man

Muslim Israelis

Muslims constitute more than 15 percent of the Israeli population. Most of them are Palestinians whose families lived in Israel prior to 1948. Muslim citizens enjoy full legal and political equality in

A group of Muslims gather for prayer in front of the Dome of the Rock on the Temple Mount.

Muslim houses of worship are called mosques. Many **mosques** are ornately decorated and adorned with Arabic inscriptions.

Israel but often find it difficult living in a Jewish state. Their holidays, dress, and customs are different from those of the Jewish majority. They generally live in separate neighborhoods from Jews and send their children to separate schools. Many Muslim Israelis feel solidarity with Palestinians living in the occupied territories. They oppose many of Israel's political policies.

Nazareth, Haifa, and Jerusalem have large Arab populations. Jaffa, part of Tel Aviv-Jaffa, was historically an Arab town, as was Acre outside of Haifa. Many Arabs also live in Galilee in northern Israel.

About 10 percent of Israel's Muslims are Bedouins, members of an ancient nomadic group. Israeli Bedouins traditionally lived in the Negev Desert, traveling from place to place with their herds of camels, goats, and sheep. In modern, industrial Israel, Bedouins often find it difficult to roam freely with their animals. More and more, Bedouins are settling in permanent towns. Many work in industries such as tourism, commerce, and farming.

A Closer Look at Islam

Muslims, the second-largest religious group in Israel, practice the Islamic faith. Islam was founded on the Arabian Peninsula in the 600s C.E. by the prophet Muhammad. The Islamic God is called Allah. The Islamic holy book is called the Quran. Muslims follow five basic practices called the Five Pillars of Islam. These practices are

- Acknowledging that there is no God but Allah and that Muhammad is his messenger
- Praying to Allah five times a day, facing the holy city of Mecca in Saudi Arabia
- Giving alms, or charity, to the poor
- Fasting from dawn to sunset during the month of Ramadan, the ninth month of the Islamic calendar
- Making a pilgrimage to Mecca at least once in a lifetime

An Armenian Orthodox priest at the Church of the Holy Sepulcher. Although the Christian population in Israel is small, many sites in the country are holy to Christians worldwide.

Israelis of Other Faiths

Only about 2 percent of Israelis are Christians. Many of them work for religious organizations, such as the Greek Orthodox Church and the Armenian Church. Many sites in Israel and the disputed territories are holy to Christians. Examples include the Church of the Holy Sepulcher in Jerusalem and the Church of the Nativity in Bethlehem. These sites are administered by Christian organizations and attract many Christian tourists. Thus, Israel has a strong Christian presence and flavor, although few Israelis are actually Christian.

About 3 percent of Israelis belong to other faiths. The majority of them are Druzes, members of a secretive Middle Eastern sect. This faith is related to Islam but has many distinct features. Druzes speak Arabic. They mostly live in villages in northern Israel. Other religious groups have small communities in Israel. These groups include the Baha'i, the Samaritans, and the Circassians.

A Jerusalem street cafe

Urban and Rural Life

About 91 percent of Israelis live in urban areas. Israel's biggest cities are Jerusalem, Tel Aviv-Jaffa, and Haifa. People in Israeli cities live much like urban dwellers in the United States. They hold jobs at banks, schools, hospitals, stores, and factories. They live in apartment buildings and private houses. They travel by foot, car, bus, and taxicab through the city streets. After work, urban Israelis like to relax at nightclubs and cafes. They gather together to enjoy sporting events, live music, theater, and other pastimes.

Just 9 percent of Israelis live in rural areas—in small villages and farming communities. More than half of these rural dwellers live in special communities called kibbutzim (singular: kibbutz) and moshavim (singular: moshav). Israel's first kibbutz, founded by Zionist pioneers, was established at Degania near Lake Kinneret in 1909. Originally, Degania and other early kibbutzim were farming communities. Later, many kibbutzim branched into other business areas, such as manufacturing, food processing, and tourism.

On a kibbutz, there is no private property. All land, buildings, and factories are owned in common. Members, called kibbutzniks, work together to make their businesses succeed. In exchange for their labor, the kibbutz provides members with food, housing, medical care, schooling, and other services. Although most kibbutzniks live in private homes with their families, they all share many facilities, such as dining halls and libraries. Kibbutzim operate democratically. Members elect officers and vote on important community issues. Most kibbutzim have between 300 and 400 members. In total about 120,000 Israelis live on approximately 270 kibbutzim throughout the nation.

All members of a **kibbutz,** even the teens and children, help out with the work. Here, two young women tend to the chickens on Kibbutz Ein Gedi.

Moshavim are generally agricultural communities. They differ from kibbutzim in that members own private homes and farms. They do not share property or living facilities. Although moshavim members live independently, they work together to market and sell their crops and other products. By selling their goods together, members receive higher prices than they would on their own. Approximately 185,000 Israelis belong to about 450 moshavim across Israel.

> If you'd like to find out more about the people of Israel, including Jews, Muslims, and other groups, go to vgsbooks.com.

◎ Settlers in the Disputed Territories

Approximately 230,000 Israelis live in the disputed territories of Gaza, the Golan Heights, and the West Bank. They occupy about 195 small settlements interspersed throughout these regions. The settlements are scattered amid larger Arab cities and towns, with some 3.2 million Arab residents in all. Being located in the heart of the disputed territories, these settlements are particularly vulnerable to terror attacks. Palestinians oppose the existing settlements and their expansion, and the settlements are often at the center of the Israeli-Arab debate.

Yet Israelis continue to move to the territories. The number of settlers has roughly doubled since 1993. Israelis live in the disputed territories for several reasons: Compared to many other places in Israel, housing is inexpensive there. In addition, the West Bank and the Golan Heights have some of the richest farmland in the region. The territories also hold many holy sites—the land is considered sacred to Jews. Finally, the Israeli government encourages settlements, which help buffer Israel from invasion.

A Jewish family works the fields on their West Bank farm near Jericho. Fertile land draws many Israelis to the occupied territories.

Third-grade students at a Jewish school in Ashqelon **study the Talmud.**

◉ Education

Israel places a high value on education. The adult literacy rate—the proportion of Israelis who can read and write—is 95 percent. All Israeli children between age five and eighteen receive free education. School attendance is required through age sixteen. The state funds both Jewish schools, in which the language of instruction is Hebrew, and Arab schools, in which the language of instruction is Arabic.

In the Jewish system, parents can send their children to either secular (nonreligious) or religious schools. Both kinds of schools teach academic courses, but religious schools also emphasize Jewish studies. Many Orthodox Jewish parents choose to send their children to private religious schools.

Most Islamic and Druze parents sent their children to Arab schools. In addition to their standard academic studies, students at these schools learn about Arab history and culture. They also receive some religious instruction. Students at all Israeli schools—Jewish and Arab, religious and secular—also learn English in the classroom.

Israel has many highly regarded colleges and universities. Examples include Hebrew University of Jerusalem, Tel Aviv University, Haifa University, Ben-Gurion University of the Negev, the Technion-Israel

BECOMING AN ISRAELI

Moving to Israel and becoming an Israeli citizen is called "making aliyah." *Aliyah* is a Hebrew word that means "going up"—and this term often accurately describes the move to Israel, especially for those Jews who were persecuted in their home countries. The Israeli government and other organizations help Jews from around the world make aliyah. They also run programs to help the immigrants (olim) obtain jobs, housing, and education.

Institute of Technology, the Weizmann Institute of Science, and the Open University of Israel. Students don't generally enter these schools right after high school. Instead, eighteen-year-old Israelis are required to serve in the military for two years (women) or three years (men). Thus, most college students in Israel are older than twenty. Approximately half of Israelis ages twenty to twenty-four are enrolled at one of the nation's universities or colleges.

Israel welcomes thousands of immigrants each year, and many arrive with no knowledge of Hebrew, the nation's primary language. Most immigrants are also unfamiliar with Israeli history, culture, and politics. To help immigrants find jobs and adjust to Israeli life, the government offers many adult education programs. There, students receive Hebrew lessons, job training, and courses on Israeli culture, history, and citizenship. Many immigrants receive this training when they enter the IDF. Other immigrants attend *ulpans*, special schools that offer intensive Hebrew study.

◉ Health Care

Israel has an excellent health-care system, characterized by top-quality hospitals, a high doctor-to-patient ratio, highly regarded medical schools, and well-trained doctors and nurses. Israel's National Health Insurance Law guarantees basic health care for all citizens.

As a result of this high level of health care, Israel's infant mortality rate is very low: 7.7 deaths per 1,000 live births. Life expectancy rates are high at 77 years for men and 80 years for women. Few Israelis suffer from AIDS and other infectious diseases; rates of HIV infection are lower than European and North American figures. But Israelis tend to suffer from health problems similar to those found in the United States. Examples include heart disease and cancer.

One of Israel's most acclaimed medical institutions is the Hadassah Medical Center in Jerusalem, which encompasses schools of medicine, nursing, and pharmacology, along with two hospitals. The facility traces its roots to two American nurses who traveled to Israel in 1913 to provide medical care to mothers and children. Gradually, their small clinic grew to become the nation's premier medical center.

Magen David Adom is Israel's emergency medical service, similar to the Red Cross in the United States. It operates a network of first aid stations, ambulances, and blood banks. Many Israeli citizens work for the organization as volunteers. With the escalation of violence in Israel, Magen David Adom has played an increasing role in providing emergency medical care to Israelis.

Magen David Adom set up emergency blood banks at the Tel Aviv city hall after the September 11, 2001, terrorist attacks in the United States.

CULTURAL LIFE

In Israeli cities, young people in trendy clothing travel the streets side by side with Bedouins in traditional robes; Orthodox Jews with heavy beards, long coats, and black hats; machine-gun-toting female soldiers; sun-worshipping tourists; Arab shopkeepers; businessmen in pin-striped suits; and everything in between. What's more, these same cities may hold a mix of ultra-modern skyscrapers, bustling outdoor markets, medieval mosques, and two-thousand-year-old ruins.

With such a diversity of faiths, ethnicities, and lifestyles, and with such a long history, it's no wonder that Israel has a rich cultural life. People here express themselves in all sorts of ways. Some devote their lives to religious study. Others pursue the literary, visual, or performing arts. Yet others enjoy sports and outdoor adventure. The Israeli people celebrate many holidays. They embrace ancient traditions while also enjoying modern media, entertainment, and technology. For the visitor, a trip to Israel will reveal a fascinating array of foods and festivals, clothing, crafts, and culture.

◎ Religion in Daily Life

In Israel religion is everywhere. Jerusalem in particular is like a living religious museum. In the Old City, visitors will see Jews at prayer at the Western Wall (the remnants of the Second Temple), Muslim worshippers at the al-Aqsa Mosque, and Christians at the Church of the Holy Sepulcher. They will see people dressed in a variety of religious outfits: Orthodox Jewish men in kippas (skullcaps), *peyot* (side curls), and tallith (prayer shawls); Ethiopian Jews in long white robes; Druze men in white turbans.

Because Israel is a Jewish state, most cities and towns observe the Jewish Sabbath, called Shabbat. Every week, from Friday at sundown to Saturday at sundown, public transportation stops. Cafes and stores close their doors. People attend synagogue and eat Shabbat meals at home. They do not work. In Muslim areas such as East Jerusalem, however, business goes on as usual. The Muslims observe their Sabbath on Friday, while Christians observe theirs on Sunday.

A Jewish family celebrates a **bar miztvah,** a young man's coming-of-age ceremony, at the Western Wall.

Holidays occur frequently in Israel. Most of them are Jewish holidays. Many last for more than one day. Because Israel uses the Jewish calendar, which is based on the phases of the moon, the holidays fall on different days each year. Israel's major holidays are

ROSH HASHANAH Usually falling in September, Rosh Hashanah is the Jewish New Year. On this holiday, people eat foods such as apples dipped in honey in hopes of a sweet new year.

YOM KIPPUR Observed ten days after Rosh Hashanah, Yom Kippur is called the Day of Atonement. During this day, people ask God's forgiveness for their sins. The holiday is marked by fasting and prayer.

SUKKOT Falling in September or October, Sukkot is a harvest festival. On this holiday, people build outdoor shelters made of branches and leaves, just like those built by the Israelites after their escape from Egypt. Some people live in these shelters for a week.

SIMCHAT TORAH Usually falling in October, Simchat Torah marks the end of the annual cycle of Torah readings in the synagogue. People attend special religious services on this day.

HANUKKAH Also called the Festival of Lights, Hanukkah is usually celebrated in December. This holiday honors the Maccabean revolt against Greek rulers in the 100s B.C.E. During this eight-day holiday, Israelis light candles each evening. This ritual recalls a miracle in the Second Temple, where oil enough for only one day burned for eight days.

TU B'SHEVAT Falling in January or February, Tu B'Shevat is the new year for trees in Israel. Israelis plant many trees during this holiday.

Children planting trees on Tu B'Shevat

PURIM Generally falling in March, Purim commemorates the Jewish escape from a plot by the wicked Persian king Haman, as recounted in the Book of Esther in the Bible. It is a festive holiday complete with costumes, noisemakers, and celebrations.

PASSOVER Also called Pesach, Passover commemorates the Exodus from Egypt. During this weeklong holiday, usually falling in April, Jews do not eat leavened bread, because the Israelites ate only unleavened bread as they wandered in the desert. Jews also hold seders, special Passover meals recalling the time of slavery in Egypt and the Exodus.

The Passover meal is called a **seder.** During this meal, people sing songs, say prayers, and eat symbolic foods.

YOM HA'SHOAH This holiday generally falls in April. It is dedicated to the memory of the six million Jews killed in the Holocaust. On this solemn day, people light candles, lower flags to half-mast, and observe two minutes of silence in remembrance of Holocaust victims.

YOM HAZIKARON Also called Remembrance Day, this holiday honors the soldiers who died in all of Israel's wars. The holiday usually falls in April or May. Like Yom Ha'Shoah, it is a solemn day filled with tributes to those who have died.

YOM HA'ATZMAUT Falling in April or May, Yom Ha'atzmaut is Israel's Independence Day. It commemorates the establishment of the State of Israel on May 14, 1948. People celebrate with fireworks, parades, and picnics.

LAG B'OMER Usually held in May, Lag B'Omer commemorates the Bar Kokhba uprising against Rome in 132 C.E. It is a joyous holiday complete with bonfires, games, singing, and dancing.

Jerusalem Day

JERUSALEM DAY Held in May, this holiday commemorates the reunification of the city of Jerusalem, which occurred during the Six-Day War in 1967. Many Israelis visit Jerusalem on this day to pray at the Western Wall.

SHAVUOT Held in May or June, Shavuot commemorates the giving of the Torah and the Ten Commandments on Mount Sinai. People observe this holiday with Torah readings. It is also a harvest celebration. People often decorate their homes and synagogues with fruits, greenery, and flowers on Shavuot.

TISHAH B'AV This holiday, held in July or August, is the anniversary of the destruction of the First and Second Temples in Jerusalem. It is a day of bereavement, marked by fasting and prayer.

Many ethnic groups in Israel observe other holidays. For example, the day after Passover, Jews of Moroccan descent celebrate a holiday called Mimouna, which honors the renewal of nature and it blessings. In November, Jews from Ethiopia observe a holiday called Sigd. On this day in Ethiopia, Jews expressed their longing to return to Israel. In Israel, celebrants give thanks for having arrived.

Muslim Israelis also celebrate many holidays. The most important is Ramadan, held during the ninth month of the Islamic calendar. This calendar, like the Jewish calendar, is based on the moon. Therefore Ramadan falls at a different time each year. During the monthlong holiday, Muslims fast every day from dawn until sunset. Evenings are devoted to prayer. At the end of Ramadan, people hold a big feast called Eid al-Fitr.

Christian holidays are important in Israel, even though only a small fraction of Israelis are Christian. But, especially on Christmas and Easter, Christian pilgrims and tourists visit Israel from all over the world. They come to worship and to see places that were important in Jesus' life.

> Learn more about Israeli cultural life at vgsbooks.com, where you'll find links to websites that feature information about various customs, recipes, holidays, music, art, and more.

A Taste of Israel

Israel's food reflects the diverse origins of its people. Since Israel is in the Mideast, and many citizens came to Israel from nearby nations, Middle Eastern food is Israel's most common cuisine. Examples include cooked meat dishes (usually lamb) such as *shwarma* and

SHAKSHUKA

Shakshuka is a popular Israeli dish. It originated with Sephardic Jews in North Africa, who brought the recipe with them to Israel. The dish is a tasty mix of eggs, tomatoes, and onions. For a variation on the recipe, sauté a minced clove of garlic or three or four slices of red pimento with the onion. Serves 4.

1 large onion, finely chopped   4 eggs

cooking oil   salt and pepper to taste

6 medium tomatoes   paprika

1. In a large frying pan, sauté onion in oil until lightly browned.
2. Grate tomatoes on the largest holes of a grater.
3. Mix grated tomatoes and onion; cover and cook over low heat for 25 minutes.
4. Remove cover and break eggs over surface.
5. Stir gently to break yolks.
6. Cover and cook for 3 or 4 minutes until eggs are set.
7. Sprinkle with salt and pepper and paprika. Serve hot.

shashlik. Baba ghanoush, an eggplant puree, is also popular. Falafel, deep-fried balls of ground chickpeas, is generally eaten inside small flat loaves of pita bread. Tahini is a tasty sesame seed spread. Halva is candy made from ground sesame seeds and honey.

In addition to Middle Eastern nations, other countries have contributed foods to the Israeli diet. For example, baklava, a sweet dessert made with nuts and honey, comes originally from Greece. Sweet, strong Turkish coffee has its origins in Turkey—of course. The Ashkenazi Jews brought their own foods to Israel from Eastern Europe. Examples include gefilte fish (ground fish mixed with eggs, matzo meal, and seasonings), blintzes (thin pancakes filled with meat, cheese, or fruit and sautéed), challah (a special holiday bread), and kugel (baked noodle or potato pudding). Israelis eat potato pancakes called latkes on Hanukkah, three-cornered pastries called hamantaschen on Purim, and

Challah

unleavened bread called matzo on Passover—just as many of their ancestors did in Europe. On Shabbat many Israelis eat a heavy stew called *cholent.* Containing meat, beans, potatoes, and vegetables, the stew can be prepared ahead of time and simmered over a low flame during Shabbat, when work is forbidden.

Israelis eat a lot of fresh foods, such as fruits, eggs, and salads. They usually eat big breakfasts and lunches and light dinners. Many Jewish Israelis keep kosher, which involves following biblical dietary laws. Under these laws, eating certain meats, such as pork and shellfish, is

Outdoor markets in Israel are packed with fresh fruits and vegetables. The Israeli diet includes a large amount of produce.

forbidden. Dairy foods must be eaten separately from meat. Many Israelis use two sets of dishes—one for dairy meals and one for meat meals. Most Israeli restaurants follow these laws.

Language and Literature

Hebrew and Arabic are Israel's official languages, but Hebrew is used most often. It is used in courts of law, government offices, and most workplaces. All government documents are published in Hebrew. Most major newspapers, magazines, and books are printed in Hebrew as well.

A large portion of Israelis—specifically the Muslim population—speak Arabic, the nation's other official language. In Muslim areas like East Jerusalem, most people speak Arabic at home, work, and school. English is also widely spoken in Israel, as are Yiddish (a language of European Jews), Russian, and other languages native to Israel's many immigrants. To accommodate its multilingual population, the Israeli government publishes Arabic and English translations of many official documents. Clerks in courts and government offices provide language interpretation services for citizens who don't speak Hebrew. Many Israeli street signs are written in Hebrew, Arabic, and English. Many newspapers and magazines are printed in these languages as well. Israeli television and radio offer Hebrew, Arabic, and English programming.

Hebrew was the language of the ancient Israelites. Their Bible was written in Hebrew. So were most of the Dead Sea Scrolls. After the bulk of the Jews were expelled from Judea in C.E. 135, they gradually spread across the Middle East, the Mediterranean area, and Europe. They naturally adopted the languages of their new countries. They used Hebrew only for scholarly and religious writing. It was no longer spoken, except during religious services. The language was nearly dormant for almost 1,700 years.

INTRODUCTION TO HEBREW

Hebrew, the primary language of Israel, is related to Arabic, Aramaic, and other Middle Eastern languages. It has its own alphabet, which contains twenty-two letters. It is written from right to left—the opposite of English. Here are a few common Hebrew words and phrases, transliterated into the Roman alphabet, and with their English meanings:

HEBREW	ENGLISH
bat	daughter
ben	son
be'vakasha	please
boker tov	good morning
ken	yes
lo	no
shalom	hello/good-bye; peace
toda	thank you

With the Zionist movement, however, Hebrew was revived. A man named Eliezer Ben-Yehuda, born in Lithuania, emigrated to Palestine in 1881. He set about making Hebrew into a living language once again. He coined new Hebrew words for modern items and ideas, established a Hebrew language periodical, and created several Hebrew dictionaries. After World War I, Great Britain recognized Hebrew as an official language of Palestine, along with Arabic and English. With Jews arriving from so many different nations, Hebrew became a unifying force in Israel's early days. The language grew and spread. From some 8,000 words in biblical times, modern Hebrew has more than 120,000 words.

Hebrew-language presses have flourished in Israel, creating a rich literary tradition. The Institute for the Translation of Hebrew Literature, established in 1962, has helped distribute the best of Israeli writing throughout the world. Israeli novelist Shmuel Yosef Agnon won the Nobel Prize for Literature in 1966. More contemporary Israeli writers include Amos Oz, David Grossman, A. B. Yehoshua, and Aharon Appelfeld.

Amos Oz

◉ Arts and Entertainment

The visual arts are also vibrant and strong in Israel, dating to the days of the early Zionists. The nation's oldest arts organization is the Bezalel Academy of Arts and Crafts, founded in 1906. Jerusalem's first major art exhibition was held in 1921. Each wave of immigration has brought new artists—and new artistic styles—to the country. For example, a style called German expressionism, which features bold, emotionally intense, and often jarring images, entered the nation's artistic arena with the arrival of German Jews fleeing the Nazis in the 1930s. The nation's artists have explored themes such as Israeli independence, the Holocaust, Judaism, and the Arab-Israeli conflict. Several acclaimed art museums, including the Tel Aviv Museum of Art and the Haifa Museum, exhibit both contemporary and historic works.

Musically, Israel has a strong folk tradition. Folk songs tell of biblical days, pioneer life, and hopes for peace. Many songs have European origins, while others have Eastern roots. Israel also has rock bands and pop singers, similar to those heard in the United States. Klezmer music, a

Pioneers,
all work as one.
Work as one, all
pioneers.
Peace shall be
for all the world.
All the world
shall be for peace.

—from "Zum Gali Gali,"
an early Zionist
folk song

Klezmer musicians perform at a Purim parade.

lively, jazzy style with its roots in Eastern Europe, is also popular in Israel.

Classical music thrives in Israel. In the 1930s, hundreds of professional musicians streamed into Israel from Europe. Orchestras were soon formed, beginning with the Palestine Philharmonic Orchestra (later called the Israel Philharmonic) in 1936. More professional groups followed, including the Jerusalem Symphony Orchestra, the New Israel Opera, and the Israel Chamber Orchestra. The musical community got another infusion of talent in the 1990s, with the arrival of hundreds of professional musicians from the former Soviet Union. Some of the world's greatest classical musicians are Israelis. Violinists Pinchas Zuckerman and Itzhak Perlman are two of the most famous examples.

Like folk songs, folk dance is extremely popular in Israel. Ordinary Israelis often gather for informal folk dance sessions, while professional troupes perform at annual folk festivals. Israeli folk dance combines many different traditions. Eastern Europeans brought the hora to Israel. Originating in Romania, the hora is a circle dance in which participants link arms. Middle Eastern Jews contributed the *debka*, a dance characterized by foot-stomping male dancers lined up in a row. Modern folk troupes have added jazz, Latin, and African styles to the mix. Several major Israeli dance companies specialize in non-folk styles, such as ballet and modern dance.

Israel boasts six professional repertory theaters and dozens of regional companies. The Habimah, based in Tel Aviv since 1932, is Israel's national theater. The Gesher Theater performs mostly Russian-language productions, while another troupe performs works

The **Gesher Theater company** was founded in 1991 by immigrants from the former Soviet Union.

for children. Some Israeli theater companies stage famous Broadway musicals—with all words and lyrics translated into Hebrew.

Filmmaking got its start in Israel in the early years of independence. The first Israeli filmmakers tackled themes such as the Holocaust and immigrant life. Many modern filmmakers have grappled with the Arab-Israeli conflict. Several institutions promote Israeli filmmaking and film studies. They include the Israel Film Center, the Spielberg Film Archive at Hebrew University, and the Jerusalem Cinematheque.

Several radio and television stations operate in Israel, providing programming in Hebrew, Arabic, and English. The Israel Defense Force radio station broadcasts news and music around the clock. Cable TV offers programming from Europe, Asia, and the United States.

Sports and Recreation

Like people everywhere, Israelis love sports, games, and outdoor recreation. Favorite recreational activities include rafting on the Jordan River, rock climbing in the Negev, and fishing on Lake Kinneret. Hiking is also very popular. The most popular spectator sports in Israel are soccer and basketball. Maccabi-Tel Aviv is a championship basketball team with a strong record both inside Israel and in European competition.

The Maccabiah Games, sometimes called the Jewish Olympics, are held every four years in the impressive 60,000-seat Ramat Gan Stadium outside Tel Aviv. The games attract Jewish athletes from all over the world—many of them tops in their sport. Americans Kerri Strug (gymnastics) and Lenny Krayzelburg (swimming) are two recent examples. The first Maccabiah Games were held in 1932—with 390 athletes and fourteen nations competing. By 2001 the games had grown to include more than 5,000 athletes from more than fifty nations. Athletes compete in more than forty events, including basketball, swimming, track and field contests, and tennis.

A U.S. track and field athlete gears up for a race at the Maccabiah Games.

THE ECONOMY

During its early years of statehood, Israel was very poor. It was more than half desert and had little land under cultivation. It also had little industry, few natural resources, and a limited supply of water. Neighboring Arab countries were hostile to Israel and refused to trade with the new nation. What's more, the thousands of new immigrants flooding into the country after 1948 needed food, housing, and social services. The nation was at first hard-pressed to provide for all its citizens' needs.

But most of these newcomers came to Israel with job skills, education, and enthusiasm for their new homeland. Israel's early citizens quickly set about building their nation's industry, roads, cities, and farms. Other nations, especially the United States, provided financial assistance to Israel as it developed.

Over the next fifty years, Israel steadily grew from a poor, rural nation into a world leader in technology, business, and finance. By the early twenty-first century, Israel enjoyed a strong economy and a high standard of living. In 2002 it ranked twenty-second in the world in per capita gross domestic product (GDP; the value of all goods and services produced in a country). The average Israeli worker earned about $1,500 per month.

But Israel still faces many economic challenges. The nation's unemployment rate is approximately 9 percent—higher than in the United States but comparable to many nations in Western Europe. Other economic struggles include a trade deficit (higher imports than exports); high foreign debt; and, because the nation is embroiled in ongoing military conflict, a high defense budget.

The Service Sector

Approximately 70 percent of Israel's citizens work in the service sector, including financial and business services, retail trade, transportation, communications, and community and social services. Government work is also part of the service sector—nearly one-third of Israelis hold jobs with the government.

Mud-covered tourists are a common sight on the shores of the Dead Sea. The mud from this salty lake is said to rejuvenate the skin.

SALT AND MUD

The Dead Sea is a popular tourist spot. Many resorts line its waters. Visitors often like to cover their bodies with mineral-rich Dead Sea mud, which is said to be good for the skin. Dead Sea salt is also thought to have healing properties. It is sold around the world as a therapeutic bath salt.

Tourism is a very important part of the service sector. With its diverse religious and historic heritage, warm weather, sunny beaches, and fascinating archaeological sites, Israel is a magnet for tourists. In the late 1990s, more than two million foreign visitors came to Israel each year. They contributed about $2.6 billion a year to the nation's economy. When suicide bombings increased in the early 2000s, however, tourism in Israel fell off drastically, hurting the economy.

◉ Industrial Jobs

Approximately 28 percent of Israelis work in construction, mining, or manufacturing. The construction business fluctuates with immigration and the demand for new housing. The mining business has always been strong in Israel. Many companies extract salt, bromine, magnesium, and potash from the Dead Sea. Phosphates, copper, clay, and gypsum are mined in the Negev Desert.

For many decades, Israel has manufactured textiles, fertilizers, pesticides, chemicals, and plastic and metal products. Many factories and processing plants are located on kibbutzim. Israel is a world leader in diamond cutting and polishing. Rough diamonds are imported to Israel from South Africa. After processing, the diamonds are exported around the world.

The Israeli high-tech industry is strong and growing. In fact, many Israeli firms are among the best in the world in areas such as medical electronics, agro-technology (farm-related technology), computer software, telecommunications, satellite technology, and Internet security. Many high-tech businesses are located in Petach Tikva, a suburb of Tel Aviv-Jaffa. This area has been likened to California's Silicon Valley—the center of high technology in the United States.

Because war and terrorism are a constant threat, Israel has developed its own weapons industry. Products include the Uzi submachine gun, tanks, and missile systems. These products are used by the IDF as well as exported to other nations.

 Visit vgsbooks.com for up-to-date information about Israel's economy and a converter where you can learn how many Israeli shekels are in one U.S. dollar.

Agriculture

The first Zionist pioneers made their living by farming. This was no easy task in such a dry, barren land. Israel's first farms were very small. Over the years, however, Israelis studied irrigation and agricultural science. They successfully brought water from northern areas to irrigate the desert south. They put more and more acres under cultivation. The amount of farmland in Israel more than doubled between 1948 and 1997. In modern Israel, about 17 percent of the land is arable, or suitable for farming. Modern Israel produces almost all the food it needs to feed its people.

Many crops, such as these olives, are harvested by hand in rural Israel.

Dates, nuts, apricots, and figs are just a few of the food crops raised and sold in Israel.

In the early years of statehood, farming was Israel's primary industry. In modern times, with the growth of the industrial and service sectors, farming has shrunk as a percentage of Israel's GDP. In 2000 approximately 2.5 percent of Israelis worked in farming, forestry, or fishing. Depending on region, Israeli farmers grow melons, dates, figs, apricots, strawberries, kiwis, mangoes, grapes, bananas, apples, and citrus fruits. Other common crops are tomatoes, wheat, cucumbers, olives, tobacco, and cotton. Some farmers grow roses, carnations, and other flowers. Many raise chickens, dairy cattle, sheep, goats, and pigs. Some farmers breed fish in artificial ponds. Others harvest trees for lumber and other products.

Many students from around the world work at kibbutzim as volunteers. This work allows young people to experience Israeli life up close—and in more depth than the typical Israeli tourist. For more information on kibbutzim and volunteering, visit vgsbooks.com for links to the Israel Aliyah Center and the Kibbutz Program Center.

The Future

Israel faces a difficult and unsettling future. Although it is a strong and prosperous democracy, its ongoing struggles with the Palestinians threaten to undermine its future security and success. Its citizens worry about war and suicide bombings on a daily basis. Yet life goes on in Israel. Despite war and terrorism, children go to school, parents go to work, families observe Shabbat and holidays, immigrants continue to arrive in Israel from nations around the world.

Israel is a nation of fighters. Many of its founders were poor, homeless, and desperate. Many had survived the Holocaust. Yet these pioneers accomplished great things. They planted forests in the desert. They built roads, farms, schools, and cities. They revived an ancient language. They defended their nation against much larger armies and established a democracy while surrounded by dictators.

And Israelis will continue to fight and to hope—as the Israeli national anthem says—"To be a free nation in our land / The land of Zion and Jerusalem."

A man flies an Israeli flag in honor of Jerusalem Day. An Islamic minaret stands in the background. Israel is a land of many cultures that continue to work toward a state of peaceful coexistence.

C. 1800 B.C.E.	Abraham and the Hebrews settle in Canaan.
C. 1200 B.C.E.	Moses leads the Israelites out of slavery in Egypt (the Exodus), followed by forty years of wandering in the desert.
C. 1020 B.C.E.	The Israelites form a monarchy and choose Saul as their king.
C. 960 B.C.E.	King Solomon builds the First Temple.
C. 721 B.C.E.	The Assyrians conquer the northern part of Israel; Judah remains independent.
586 B.C.E.	Judah is conquered by the Babylonians.
538–515 B.C.E.	Jews return to Jerusalem and build the Second Temple.
166–161 B.C.E.	The Maccabee brothers lead a revolt against Syrian rule.
63 B.C.E.	Jerusalem is captured by the Roman general Pompey.
0 B.C.E.	Jesus of Nazareth is born in Bethlehem.
C.E. 132	Simon Bar Kokhba leads an uprising against Rome.
C.E. 136	Emperor Hadrian expels the Jews from Judea, and the Diaspora begins. Judea is renamed Palestine.
C.E. 637	Arab armies conquer Palestine.
1095	European knights begin the Crusades to capture Palestine from the Arabs.
1517	The Ottoman Turks take control of Palestine.
1897	Theodor Herzl convenes the First Zionist Congress in Basel, Switzerland.
1901	The Jewish National Fund is founded. Its initial goal is to raise money for the purchase of land in Israel.
1906	The Bezalel Academy of Arts and Crafts is founded.
1909	Degania Kibbutz is founded near Lake Kinneret. Tel Aviv is founded on the Mediterranean coast.
1917	With the Balfour Declaration, Great Britain pledges support for a Jewish homeland in Palestine.
1918	World War I ends. The Ottoman Empire is defeated.
1922	The British mandate begins in Palestine.
1932	The first Maccabiah Games are held in Israel.

1939-1945 The Nazis kill six million European Jews (the Holocaust) during World War II.

1947 The first Dead Sea Scrolls are discovered.

1948 Israel proclaims its independence. It is immediately invaded by five Arab nations.

1950 The Knesset passes the Law of Return, granting Israeli citizenship to any Jew who desires it.

1956 Israel seizes the Sinai Peninsula but later withdraws its troops.

1964 Israel completes the National Water Carrier, a major water transportation network.

1967 War breaks out with Egypt, Jordan, and Syria. It ends in six days.

1973 Syria and Egypt attack Israel on Yom Kippur.

1978 Egyptian president Anwar Sadat and Israeli prime minister Menachem Begin hold peace negotiations at Camp David in Maryland.

1982 After prolonged attacks against Israel's northern border, Israeli troops attack PLO fighters in southern Lebanon.

1985 The first Ethiopian Jews are airlifted to Israel.

1987 Palestinians in the disputed territories begin an intifada (uprising).

1989 Soviet Jews begin a mass immigration to Israel.

1993 Prime minister Yitzhak Rabin and PLO leader Yasser Arafat sign the Oslo Accords.

1995 Yitzhak Rabin is assassinated by a Jewish extremist.

1996 The Palestinian National Authority is organized.

1998 Israel celebrates its fiftieth anniversary.

2001 Suicide bombings increase inside Israel.

2002 The Israel Defense Force (IDF) invades Palestinian towns to apprehend terrorists. Israel begins construction on a security wall along the West Bank border.

COUNTRY NAME State of Israel

AREA 8,000 square miles (20,720 square km), excluding disputed territories

MAIN LANDFORMS Coastal plain, Judeo-Galilean Highlands, Jordan Rift, Negev Desert

HIGHEST POINT Mount Meron, 3,963 feet (1,208 m) above sea level

LOWEST POINT Dead Sea 1,300 feet (396 m) below sea level

MAJOR RIVERS Besor, Hadera, Jordan, Qarn, Qishon, Yarqon

ANIMALS badgers, boars, foxes, gazelles, hares, hyenas, ibexes, jackals, weasels, wildcats, wolves

CAPITAL CITY Jerusalem

OTHER MAJOR CITIES Tel Aviv-Jaffa, Haifa, Eilat, Beersheba, Nazareth

OFFICIAL LANGUAGES Hebrew, Arabic

MONETARY UNIT new Israeli shekel. 1 shekel = 100 agorot

ISRAELI CURRENCY

Israel's monetary unit is the new Israeli shekel (NIS). Shekels, or *shekelim*, are divided into 100 agorot. Israel issues 10 and 50 agorot coins and 1 and 5 NIS coins. Paper currency is issued in 5, 10, 20, 50, 100, and 200 NIS notes.

The Israeli flag features a white background with a blue Magen David ("shield of David") between two horizontal blue bands. The flag is based on the design of the Jewish tallith, or prayer shawl. The Magen David, also called the star of David or Jewish star, is a six-pointed star. Because of its name, some people think the symbol dates to King David's time (circa 1000 B.C.E). It actually emerged as a Jewish symbol much later—its first use by Jews can be traced to the C.E. 500s. In the late 1800s, Theodor Herzl adopted the symbol for the Zionist movement and a new Jewish state.

Israel's national anthem is "Hatikva," which means "the hope." The words were written by Naftali Herz Imber, a Polish Jew who moved to Palestine in 1882. Samuel Cohen, an immigrant from Moldavia, set the words to music. The lyrics express the hope of the Jewish people to return to their homeland in Israel. Below is the English translation of one verse.

Hatikva
As long as deep in the heart
The soul of a Jew yearns,
And forward to the East,
To Zion, an eye looks,
Our hope will not be lost,
The hope of two thousand years,
To be a free nation in our land,
The land of Zion and Jerusalem.

For a link where you can listen to Israel's national anthem, "Hatikva," go to vgsbooks.com.

YAACOV AGAM (b. 1928) Israeli-born Yaacov Agam attended the Bezalel Academy of Arts and Crafts in Jerusalem and the Atelier d'Art Abstrait in Paris. Called the father of kinetic (moving) art, Agam has created a variety of abstract work, including kinetic sculpture, computer art, electronic art, and touchable paintings and sculptures. His work has been exhibited around the world.

SHMUEL YOSEF AGNON (1888–1970) Shmuel Yosef Agnon is one of Israel's most famous fiction writers. He was born in Galicia (in modern-day Ukraine and Poland) and moved to Israel in 1908. Most of his works deal with Jewish life in turn-of-the-last-century Galicia or the lives of Zionist pioneers. In 1966 he won the Nobel Prize for literature. He also received the Israel Prize, Israel's top civilian honor, on two occasions.

DAVID BEN-GURION (1886–1973) David Ben-Gurion was Israel's first prime minister and first defense minister. He was born in Plonsk in modern-day Poland and moved to Palestine in 1906. An early Zionist leader, Ben-Gurion helped establish the Mapai (Israel Workers' Party), the Histradrut (Israel's largest trade union), and the state of Israel itself. He served as prime minister and defense minister from 1948 to 1953 and again from 1955 to 1963. In these positions, he oversaw the nation during its early growth and several military conflicts.

ELIEZER BEN-YEHUDA (1858–1922) Born in Lithuania, Eliezer Ben-Yehuda was responsible for reviving the Hebrew language. An early Zionist, Ben-Yehuda was determined to make Hebrew the national language of Israel. He moved to Jerusalem in 1881, where he founded several organizations dedicated to the revival of Hebrew. He published a Hebrew newspaper and wrote several Hebrew dictionaries. He also coined new Hebrew words for objects and ideas that did not exist when Hebrew was used in ancient times.

DAVID GROSSMAN (b. 1954) Writer David Grossman was born in Jerusalem and educated at Hebrew University. He has examined Israeli life through both fiction and nonfiction. His award-winning works have been translated into dozens of languages. Examples include *Yellow Wind* (1987), *Sea Under: Love* (1986), and *Sleeping on a Wire: Conversations with Palestinians in Israel* (1992).

THEODOR HERZL (1860–1904) Theodor Herzl was born in Hungary and worked in Austria as a journalist. Alarmed by anti-Jewish sentiment in Europe, Herzl reasoned that Jews would be free of oppression only when they had a homeland of their own. His book *The Jewish State* (1896) attracted many people to the Zionist cause. In 1897 Herzl presided over the First Zionist Congress in Basel, Switzerland. Although he died in 1904, several decades before Israel officially became a nation, Herzl is considered the country's founding father.

GOLDA MEIR (1989–1978) Golda Meir served as prime minister of Israel from 1969 to 1974. She was the only woman ever to hold this position. Meir was born in Kiev, Ukraine. She moved to Milwaukee, Wisconsin, with her family as a child and later moved to Tel Aviv. She worked for the Histradrut, Israel's major trade union, before taking positions in the Israeli government. The Yom Kippur War occurred during her term as prime minister.

ITZHAK PERLMAN (b. 1945) Tel Aviv–born Itzhak Perlman is one of the world's greatest classical musicians. He studied violin at the Juilliard School in New York and soon won international acclaim. He has appeared with nearly every major orchestra in the world, including the Israel Philharmonic. He has made dozens of recordings and often performs with other renowned musicians. In addition to classical works, Perlman frequently performs klezmer music.

YITZHAK RABIN (1922–1995) Born in Jerusalem, Yitzhak Rabin twice served as Israel's prime minister (1974–1977, 1992–1995). He also served as the IDF chief of staff, a Knesset member, Israel's ambassador to the United States, and in other positions. In 1993 Rabin signed the historic Oslo Accords with PLO leader Yasser Arafat, an agreement that earned both men (as well as Israeli foreign minister Shimon Peres) the Nobel Peace Prize. In 1995 Rabin was assassinated by a Jewish extremist who opposed his concessions to the Palestinians.

ILAN RAMON (1954–2003) Born in Tel Aviv, Ilan Ramon was Israel's first astronaut. The son of a Holocaust survivor, he studied electronics and computer engineering at Tel Aviv University, then became a fighter pilot in the Israeli Air Force. In 1997 Ramon was selected by NASA, the U.S. space agency, to serve as a payload specialist on the space shuttle *Columbia*. The shuttle was launched on January 16, 2003. Tragically, it exploded just before landing on February 1, 2003. Ramon and the six other crewmembers were killed.

HENRIETTA SZOLD (1860–1945) The daughter of a Baltimore rabbi, Henrietta Szold grew up to become a leader in the Zionist movement. Szold moved to New York, where she founded Hadassah, the National Women's Zionist Organization. It grew to become the largest Zionist organization in the world. In 1920 Szold moved to Israel, where she continued her Zionist work. During the 1930s, she devoted herself to rescuing Jewish youth from Nazi Germany and bringing them to Israel.

CHAIM TOPOL (b. 1935) Tel Aviv–born Chaim Topol is one of Israel's most famous actors. He is best known for his performance as Tevye in the film *Fiddler on the Roof* (1971). He has also played the role on the stage several times. He has acted in many films, plays, and television shows. He has also written and illustrated books. He has won numerous acting awards, including two Golden Globes.

CAESAREA Caesarea is one of Israel's premier archaeological sites. Herod, a Roman king, took control of the city in about 22 B.C.E. and built a number of grand structures there. Visitors can see an amphitheater, a bathhouse, aqueducts, and other artifacts from Herod's time. Crusaders took control of Caesarea in the C.E. 1100s, and their structures also remain, including city walls and buildings.

THE DEAD SEA The Dead Sea is one of Israel's most popular tourist sites. Visitors love to float in the sea's salty waters and cover themselves in healthful Dead Sea mud. A nearby attraction is Qumran, site of the discovery of the Dead Sea Scrolls. Ein Gedi, a lush nature preserve with beautiful pools and waterfalls, is also located near the Dead Sea.

MASADA A sheer-sided plateau near the Dead Sea, Masada was a fortress in ancient times, established by the Romans. In C.E. 66, a Jewish group called the Zealots captured the fortress and took refuge there. It is said that they eventually killed themselves rather than be captured by the Romans. Modern-day visitors can hike or take a cable car to the top of the site. There they can tour the fortress structures, including its towers, citadels, dwelling quarters, and gates.

THE NEGEV The rocky Negev Desert holds a variety of interesting attractions. Eilat, at the southern end of the desert, is the site of world-famous coral reefs. Snorkelers and scuba divers can explore a fascinating underwater world here. In the middle of the desert, the giant Maktesh Ramon crater offers great hiking and breathtaking views. Beersheba in the north has a large Bedouin population. Visitors here can learn about Bedouin culture and visit the town's colorful Bedouin market. In other parts of the Negev, visitors will encounter ancient towns, archaeological sites, and wildlife preserves.

THE OLD CITY Jerusalem's Old City is a maze of crowded and colorful streets, shops, and historic sites. The city walls were built in the 1500s, but inside the city is much older. It is divided into four quarters—Jewish, Muslim, Armenian, and Christian—and is entered via eight gates. The Old City teems with important religious sites, such as the Western Wall, the Dome of the Rock, the Temple Mount, the Via Dolorosa, and the Church of the Holy Sepulcher.

TEL AVIV-JAFFA Tel Aviv-Jaffa is where Israelis go to have fun. Located right on the Mediterranean Sea, it is a cosmopolitan city, famed for its trendy nightclubs, galleries, and cafes. The city also has beautiful sandy beaches. Those interested in history will want to tour Jaffa, the city's ancient Arab section, and visit the Diaspora Museum, which traces Jewish life from ancient to modern times. Other Tel Aviv area highlights include the bustling Carmel Market, the Tel Aviv Museum of Art, and the terrific Ramat Gan Zoo.

anti-Semitism: hostility toward or discrimination against Jews

Ashkenazim: Jews who trace their roots to Eastern Europe

cultivation: the process of farming the land

developed nation: a country with a strong industrial sector and a high standard of living

Diaspora: the scattering of Jews throughout many nations after their expulsion from Judea in C.E. 136

disputed territories: The West Bank, East Jerusalem, the Gaza Strip, and the Golan Heights—all areas that were captured by Israel during the Six-Day War. Also called the occupied territories.

Eastern: Middle Eastern or Asian in outlook, culture, and tradition

Exodus: the Israelites' escape from slavery in Egypt in the 1200s B.C.E.

gross domestic product: the value of all goods and services produced in a country during a certain time period

guerrilla warfare: unconventional warfare carried out by small groups of combatants, often involving bombings and other terrorist tactics

Israel Defense Force: Israel's army; also known as the IDF

jihad: A holy war on behalf of Islam

kibbutzim: Israeli communities in which all land, property, and business operations are owned in common. In exchange for their labor, members receive food, housing, medical care, and other services.

kosher: adhering to ancient Jewish dietary laws

mandated territory: a conquered territory ruled temporarily by a member of the League of Nations after World War I

moshavim: Israeli agricultural communities in which members join together to market and sell their crops and other products

Oriental Jews: Jews who trace their roots to the Middle East and Asia

Orthodox Jews: religious Jews who strictly follow the teachings of the Torah and the Talmud

pilgrim: someone who travels to a religious shrine or other holy place

Sephardim: Jews who trace their roots to Portugal and Spain

suicide bombers: terrorists who detonate bombs attached to their own bodies, killing themselves as well as others

Torah: the Hebrew Bible, comprised of the five books of Moses

Western: European or North American in outlook, culture, and tradition

Zionism: the international movement for a Jewish homeland in Israel

Glossary

American-Israeli Cooperative Enterprise, *Jewish Virtual Library,* **2002**
<http://www.us-israel.org> (April–June 2002)
This extensive website offers a wealth of information on Israel, with sections on Israeli history, politics, culture, and religion. The site also includes maps, statistics, and biographies of famous Israelis.

Central Intelligence Agency (CIA), "Israel," *The World Factbook,* **2001**
<http://www.odci.gov/cia/publications/factbook> (April–June 2002)
The World Factbook provides basic information on Israel's geography, people, government, economy, communications, transportation, military, and transnational issues.

***The 50 Years War: Israel and the Arabs,* dir. Brian Lapping and Norma Percy, 300 min., PBS Home Video, 1999, videocassette.**
This exhaustive two-part documentary examines the Arab-Israeli conflict from 1947 to 1998. It features extensive news footage and interviews with former soldiers, government officials, and diplomats, including U.S. president Jimmy Carter, Palestinian leader Yasser Arafat, and Israeli prime minister Golda Meir.

Hellander, Paul, Andrew Humphreys, and Neil Tilbury. *Israel and the Palestinian Territories.* **Oakland, CA: Lonely Planet Publications, 1999.**
This guidebook contains information for the visitor to Israel and the occupied territories. It examines Israeli history and culture, provides practical information for travelers, and describes major sites and attractions.

Hohenberg, John. *Israel at 50: A Journalist's Perspective.* **Syracuse: Syracuse University Press, 1998.**
This book takes a comprehensive look at Israeli politics, from independence to the current Palestinian crisis.

Shapiro, Delilah. *Israel: Triumph of the Spirit.* **New York: MetroBooks, 1997.**
Published for the state of Israel's fiftieth anniversary, this book presents a comprehensive history of Israel, beginning in ancient times. It also presents images of the people and places of modern-day Israel.

"Special Report: The Future of Israel. How Will It Survive," *Newsweek,* **April 1, 2002, 22–50.**
This series of articles details the Israeli-Palestinian crisis of 2002. Articles examine rising anti-Semitism in the Middle East and Europe, conflicting political opinions within Israel, living with the daily threat of terror in Israel, life in the occupied territories, and recent peace negotiations. It also contains an interview with Israeli prime minister Ariel Sharon and demographic and population statistics for both Israelis and Palestinians.

Selected Bibliography

State of Israel, *Israel Ministry of Foreign Affairs,* **1998**
<http://www.mfa.gov.il/mfa/home.asp> (April–June 2002)
This comprehensive site, produced by the Israeli government, provides information on all aspects of Israeli life and society, including history, government, culture, the economy, religion, and science and technology.

The Statesman's Yearbook: The Politics, Cultures, and Economies of the World 2002. **New York: Palgrave Publishers Ltd., 2001.**
This source presents a variety of statistics on Israeli society, government, industry, communications, and culture. It also includes a discussion of key historical events.

Ben Artzi-Pelossof, Noa. *In the Name of Sorrow and Hope.* **New York: Alfred A. Knopf, 1996.**

This stirring memoir was written by the nineteen-year-old granddaughter of Israeli prime minister Yitzhak Rabin. In the book, she tells of growing up in modern Israel, her grandfather's work to achieve peace, and his tragic assassination.

CNN.com In-Depth Special—Mideast: Centuries of Conflict
Website: <http://www.cnn.com/SPECIALS/2001/mideast/>

This Internet site presents a thorough examination of the Israeli-Palestinian conflict. It looks at the key issues under debate, with summaries of both Israeli and Palestinian viewpoints. It also explores the history of the conflict, key players, and key documents. Maps are included.

Finkelstein, Norman. *Theodor Herzl: Architect of a Nation.* **Minneapolis: Lerner Publications Company, 1991.**

This inspiring biography tells how Zionist pioneer Herzl rallied the Jews of Europe, met with heads of state, and set the stage for the creation of a Jewish nation in Israel.

Gresko, Marcia. *Israel.* **Minneapolis: Lerner Publications Company, 2000.**

This richly illustrated book presents Israel's many cultures, fascinating traditions, and breathtaking landscapes.

Grossman, Laurie. *Children of Israel.* **Minneapolis: Lerner Publications Company, 2001.**

Focusing on the nation's children, Israeli author and photographer Laurie Grossman explores Israel's rich history, geography, and cultural diversity.

Herzl, Theodor. *The Jewish State.* **New York: Dover Publications, 1989.**

In this historic book, Herzl outlines a step-by-step process for establishing a Jewish state. Its publication in 1896 stirred up worldwide support for Zionism.

Hintz, Martin, and Stephen Hintz. *Israel.* **Enchantment of the World Series. Danbury, CT: Children's Press, 1999.**

Written for readers ages nine through twelve, this book explores Israel's geography, wildlife, history, economics, culture, and religion. It includes detailed maps and full-color photographs.

Jerusalem Post Internet Edition
Website <http://www.jpost.com>

The *Jerusalem Post* is Israel's major English-language newspaper. Its on-line edition includes sections on national news, business, sports, culture, and community events. The paper is a good source of up-to-date information on the ongoing Israel-Palestinian conflict.

Kort, Michael G. *Yitzhak Rabin: Israel's Soldier Statesman.* **Brookfield, CT: Millbrook Press, 1996.**
As Israel's prime minister, Yitzhak Rabin worked tirelessly to negotiate a peace settlement with the Palestinians, an effort that earned him the Nobel Peace Prize. His efforts also won him many enemies—he was assassinated by a Jewish extremist who opposed his policies. This book, written for young adults, tells the story of this courageous statesman.

Maltz, Fran. *Keeping Faith in the Dust.* **Los Angeles: Alef Design Group, 1998.**
This young-adult novel tells the story of the siege of Masada, as seen through the eyes of a thirteen-year-old Jewish girl. Hannah, living near Jerusalem in the first century C.E., learns to embrace Judaism as she lives among a band of courageous martyrs fighting for Israel.

Schroeter, Daniel. *Israel: An Illustrated History.* **New York: Oxford University Children's Books, 1999.**
This well-researched book for young adults tells Israel's story through first-person accounts, quotes, archival documents, artwork, and photographs. Chapters explore Israel from ancient times through statehood and the modern era.

Slavik, Diane. *Daily Life in Ancient and Modern Jerusalem.* **Minneapolis: Lerner Publications Company, 2001.**
This title explores Jerusalem's history, from ancient to modern times. Photographs, illustrations, and interesting sidebars help shed light on this important and holy city—the heart of the Israeli nation.

Captions for photos appearing on cover and chapter openers:

Cover: The historic structures of Jerusalem's Old City draw tourists from all over the world.

pp. 4–5 A section of a mosaic of ancient Jerusalem, dating to approximately 500 C.E. The entire mosaic is called the Madaba Map. It is one of the earliest accurate maps of the region.

pp. 8–9 The Arch is one of many impressive rock formations in Timna Park, north of Eilat.

pp. 18–19 A portion of the Dead Sea Scrolls. Sections of these ancient scrolls—inscribed with Hebrew prayers and teachings—were discovered between 1947 and 1956 along the northwest shore of the Dead Sea.

pp. 36–37 Men and boys studying Jewish law

pp. 48–49 Arch of the Hurva (Ruined Synagogue) in the Jewish quarter of the Old City of Jerusalem. The synagogue was destroyed during the War of Independence. When the Israelis recovered Jerusalem in the Six Day War of 1967, they rebuilt a single arch in the ruins to commemorate the holy site and its destruction in the war.

pp. 60–61 A collection of Israeli currency